THE
PLANT LOVER'S GUIDE
TO
CLEMATIS

THE **PLANT LOVER'S GUIDE** TO
CLEMATIS

LINDA BEUTLER

TIMBER PRESS
PORTLAND, OREGON

CONTENTS

6

Why I Love Clematis

11

Designing with the Queen of Vines

39

Understanding the Genus

63
196 Clematis for the Garden

LARGE-FLOWERED HYBRIDS............................ 64

SMALL-FLOWERED HYBRIDS, SELECTIONS, AND SPECIES....................... 140

211
Growing and Propagating

WHERE TO BUY 236

WHERE TO SEE 239

FOR MORE INFORMATION..... 242

HARDINESS ZONE TEMPERATURES 244

ACKNOWLEDGMENTS 245

PHOTO CREDITS.................. 246

INDEX 247

ABOUT THE AUTHOR 254

WHY I LOVE CLEMATIS

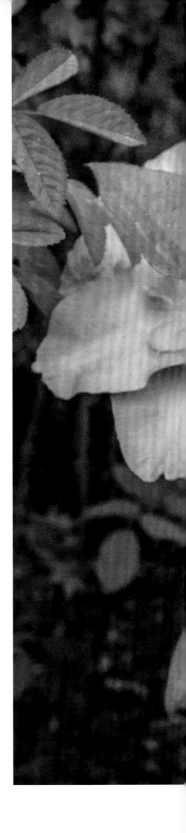

What's not to love? There are approximately 300 *Clematis* species (depending on which book you read), located on all the major continents except Antarctica. (But who knows what is under that melting ice?) The plants can be small evergreen shrublets on the South Island of New Zealand (*C. marmoraria*), herbaceous perennials from the brutal shores of Lake Baikal in Siberia (*C. integrifolia*), deciduous woodland shrubs from Korea (*C. urticifolia*), and of course vines.

Clematis 'Louise Rowe'
(Large-flowered Hybrid).

Since you asked, yes, I *do* have a favorite: *Clematis* 'Venosa Violacea' (Viticella Group).

England's only *Clematis* species, *C. vitalba*, attains enough height and weight to fell trees. There are clematis vines with no leaves (*C. afoliata*) and vines that prefer wet feet (*C. crispa*). Most clematis are proficient pollinator attractors, and some (Texas native *C. carrizoensis*, *C. glaucophylla*, *C. texensis*) are pollinated by hummingbirds. Some have fragrant blossoms (*C. montana* var. *wilsonii* hort., *C. rehderiana*). Species native to the Balearic Islands in the Mediterranean Sea flower in the winter.

Exploration and research on this far-flung genus continue apace, from Russia and China to the southeastern United States. The real miracle of *Clematis* is that taxonomists have not pulled it apart into dozens of little pieces.

No matter what your garden needs, there is likely at least one clematis to fill any niche you require. Modern large-flowered hybrids are available in any color except bright yellow and orange, and may be single, semidouble, and fully double (sometimes on the same vine at the same time). Clematis are being bred to stay short, flower over longer periods, or rebloom quickly, as well as to suit the demands of the cut flower industry.

And it is no longer a truism that a garden full of clematis must be a garden replete with arbors, pergolas, trellises, fences, and other built structures with which to hold clematis aloft. Vertical is not the only direction vining clematis will grow, and non-climbing clematis need not be strapped to a tuteur like a Victorian lady in a corset. In the wild, species clematis consort with other plants, either blooming concurrently or unwittingly adding interest in the wilderness when shrubby neighbors are merely being green.

You will notice asterisks (❋) next to some names in the 196 "clematis for the garden" entries. These plants have been included in the International Clematis Society's Clematis for Beginners list. You may safely assume any clematis making that list has been trialed all over the world and has been deemed easy to grow, dependable, and, oh yes . . . beautiful!

We are told one ought not have favorites in a collection. What utter nonsense! Such directives go against human nature. You see my favorite pictured here, 'Venosa Violacea' (Viticella Group).

DESIGNING WITH THE QUEEN OF VINES

Clematis 'Abundance'(Viticella Group) at Silver Star Vinery, Yacolt, Washington.

W

When adding clematis to your garden, do not limit yourself by thinking what size trellis you will need, how you'll afford it, and where you'll position it. It's all well and good if you *want* more man-made structures, but every woody shrub, hedge, and tree in your garden is capable of hoisting clematis where they can be seen to best advantage. Why spend ten times the cost of the clematis on the support for it, when you have plenty of living partners already in place? My only advice is to remember a clematis will attain its mature size much more quickly than a shrub or tree will, and you must give the woody plant a running start.

Given the variety of color, flower shape, bloom time, size, and habit of the clematis, the possibility for artistic expression with plant combinations is perhaps more pronounced in this genus than any other. Think of the living bones of your garden as a blank canvas upon which you paint with a palette of clematis colors and shapes.

The result of enhancing your garden by adding clematis to existing plantings without obvious artifice is a more naturalistic composition, which will appear less designed and less formal, and frees the clematis to surprise you by creating plant combinations of their own. When you allow the plants scope for their own improvisation (and they *will* improvise if not strapped to a trellis like the village drunk trussed in the stocks), your garden becomes more individual. Think of planting clematis as entering into a partnership. You provide the framework—plus water and fertilizer—and let the clematis wander, or cover the ground, or reach for the sky.

"White royal crown" indeed: *Clematis* 'Hakuokan' (Large-flowered Hybrid).

The drama of black and white: *Clematis* 'Royal Velours' (Viticella Group) in *Cornus controversa* 'Variegata'.

One good groundcover deserves another:
Clematis 'Arabella' (Integrifolia Group) with
Arctostaphylos uva-ursi 'Massachusetts'.

Brit shortlist

THE ROYAL HORTICULTURAL SOCIETY routinely trials and assesses ornamental plants for their "consistency, reliability, and excellence for ordinary garden use." The following clematis featured in this book, having been put through their paces, hold the RHS's Award of Garden Merit as of January 2015.

C. 'Abundance'
C. *alpina* 'Pamela Jackman'
C. 'Aotearoa'
C. 'Apple Blossom'
C. 'Arabella'
C. Arctic Queen 'Evitwo'
C. 'Bill MacKenzie'
C. 'Blekitny Aniol' Blue Angel
C. 'Broughton Star'
C. ×*cartmanii* 'Joe'
C. *cirrhosa* var. *purpurascens*
    'Freckles'
C. 'Comtesse de Bouchaud'
C. 'Constance'
C. 'Daniel Deronda'
C. ×*durandii*
C. 'Ernest Markham'
C. 'Étoile Violette'
C. 'Fujimusume'
C. 'Gillian Blades'
C. 'Helsingborg'
C. 'Huldine'

C. 'Jackmanii'
C. 'Madame Julia Correvon'
C. 'Markham's Pink'
C. 'Minuet'
C. 'Mrs. George Jackman'
C. 'Nelly Moser'
C. 'Niobe'
C. 'Pangbourne Pink'
C. Petit Faucon 'Evisix'
C. 'Polish Spirit'
C. 'Prince Charles'
C. 'Princess Diana'
C. 'Purpurea Plena Elegans'
C. *rehderiana*
C. 'The President'
C. 'Venosa Violacea'
C. 'Victoria'
C. 'Warszawska Nike' Midnight
    Showers
C. 'Will Goodwin'
C. Wisley 'Evipo001'

Clematis and Roses

Roses almost always look like roses. Whether demure miniature or rocketing rambler, "Rose is a rose is a rose is a rose." The same cannot be said of clematis, and yet the two genera grown together are often magnificent. Whether you prefer the subtle insinuation of herbaceous perennial clematis bells through a floribunda rose, or a plump large-flowered hybrid vine covering the bare legs of a slatternly old climbing rose, any color and texture combination can be accommodated.

  The issues to keep foremost in mind when selecting roses and clematis combinations are as follows.

Clematis 'Viola' (Large-flowered Hybrid) with roses 'Great Western' and 'Félicité Perpétue'.

Like pruning requirements. For hybrid tea and floribunda roses that are hard pruned in late winter, select clematis that also tolerate hard pruning (down to 12 inches/30 cm tall), and do not get too tall. For example, if the rose stays about 5 feet (1.5 m) tall, select a clematis, whether an herbaceous perennial or vining clematis, that will get no taller than 8 feet (2.5 m). A too-vigorous clematis will keep light from the rose leaves, and eventually the rose will decline. By contrast, if you plan to grow a large clematis into a climbing rose you rarely prune, select a clematis that does not require annual hard pruning.

Bloom time. Simply put, do you want the clematis to bloom with the rose, or pretty-up the rose while it is out of bloom? This is an especially important consideration if you grow the heirloom roses that are once-blooming. It is certainly possible to select a clematis that will begin flowering with the rose but will also continue or rebloom, once the rose has finished.

Clematis 'Andromeda' (Large-flowered Hybrid) with *Rosa* 'Robin Hood'.

Covering bare legs. If you are growing massive climbing roses that shade their own trunks and therefore lose lower leaves, shade-tolerant clematis might be an ideal solution for blatant garden nudity. Select a clematis as your coverslut that will get tall enough to cover the rose to the desired height, in a color that will suit the location. If the rose is long established, the clematis will need to be planted 3 feet (1 m) away from the crown of the rose to avoid root competition.

Does this clematis make my hips look big? Keep in mind that many of the fine new landscape roses, and most old ramblers, form decorative fruit, or hips, in the late summer and autumn, the same time many clematis rebloom. This is another texture/color partnership to bear in mind.

Structure size. Climbing roses need supporting structures. Because their only means of climbing is to fling out a long cane and hope the thorns latch onto something sturdy, no mere hydrangea or

Clematis 'Hagley Hybrid' Pink Chiffon (Large-flowered Hybrid) with *Rosa* 'Thelma'.

Clematis 'Iubileinyi-70' (Large-flowered Hybrid) and *Rosa* Monkey Business 'Jacfrara', a floribunda, partner well because they can both be hard pruned at the same time.

mock-orange (*Philadelphus*) or deutzia will hold up a mature climbing or rambling rose. If you want to grow a clematis with your climbing rose, factor in the added weight when determining what size structure you need.

Fertilizing. Nothing could be easier. Clematis respond well to any brand of organic rose and flower food where the N–P–K (nitrogen–phosphorus–potassium) formula is less than 10 for each element. If you like using alfalfa pellets on your roses, encircle your clematis crowns at the same time (but do not pile the pellets directly over the clematis canes, as one may do for roses with impunity). The only real issue is timing. Most rose manuals suggest a first feeding in April. Clematis prefer to start earlier, with a first feeding in March. If you are growing large-flowered hybrid clematis with your roses, remember to avoid fertilizing the clematis once the buds are over 2 inches (5 cm) long (this is one way to prevent the clematis plant from collapsing at bloom time). Wait for the clematis to finish blooming before fertilizing again. For clematis other than the large-flowered hybrids, you can safely fertilize the clematis whenever you feed your roses.

Fungal diseases on roses. Many types of roses, especially the hybrid tea and floribunda groups, are susceptible to black spot, powdery mildew, and rust, all fungal diseases. The prevailing wisdom has always been to grow these sorts of roses in the open without companion plants around them, to promote healthy air circulation. In a small garden, one can hardly be expected to be so accommodating, especially if you're a generalist gardener who likes lots of kinds of plants. Therefore, keep in mind that there are thousands, no, *tens* of thousands of roses on the market, and if you find one rose intolerably sickly, grub

Clematis 'Gravetye
Beauty' (Texensis
Group) in front
of *Rosa* ×*odorata*
'Mutabilis'.

To clash or not to clash: tight color harmonies are not to
everyone's taste, but try planting dangerously! *Clematis* 'Gipsy
Queen' (Large-flowered Hybrid) and *Rosa* 'La Belle Sultane'.

it out and try another. It isn't the fault of your clematis if
the rose you pair it with gets spotty. It was probably destined to be diseased anyway.

Beyond these tips, what colors and shapes you put
together is purely personal. Because of the range of laven-
ders and blues in clematis, there are some nice color con-
trasts to be had with yellow, orange, and coral roses. Some
of the best blue clematis are bells, and the texture composition of a ridged or twirled open bell with a portly old
fully double rose is one I find exciting.

If you prefer tight color harmonies, there is a clematis
to match nearly any shade of pink or burgundy in roses.
Red is more problematic since, although I am loath to
admit it, very few red clematis are truly red. Therefore, the
safest partner for a truly red rose is likely to be white, or
one of the white clematis with a red outline or bar. Being
something of a drama queen when it comes to color, with
a fully saturated red rose (such as 'Dusky Maiden'), I'd go
with a rich purple clematis with a velvety sheen, perhaps
Fleuri 'Evipo042' or 'Julka'.

Clematis in the Mixed Border

Combining clematis with deciduous or broadleaf evergreen shrubs is very little different from combining them with roses. After considerations of a personally subjective nature—your preferred colors and textures—the remaining details are purely mechanical. Care must be taken that leafy clematis with heavy vines do not overwhelm deciduous shrubs, since the shrubs do not have the advantage of photosynthesizing through the winter, the way evergreens do. Lighter weight or herbaceous perennial clematis are best for low-growing spireas, hydrangeas, barberries, and the like. Bigger shrubs and broadleaf evergreens can tolerate bigger clematis.

Clematis 'Maksymilian Kolbe' (Large-flowered Hybrid) with *Viburnum plicatum* f. *tomentosum* 'Molly Schroeder'.

Clematis 'Albina Plena' (Atragene Group) with *Buxus sempervirens* 'Variegata'.

Clematis can provide color in out-of-bloom shrubs and small trees: *Clematis* Kingfisher 'Evipo037' (Large-flowered Hybrid) in *Acer palmatum* 'Fjellheim'.

With shrubs come many variegated foliage options. Very few clematis show any variegation or distinctive leaf coloration, but there are loads of shrubs that do. Therefore, we have yet more color and texture variations to consider beyond what amounts to a relatively short bloom period for most shrubs (hydrangeas excepted, of course).

But the real advantage to growing clematis into shrubs is having those blobby lilacs, rhododendrons, weigelas, and beautyberries, with their limited season of interest, offer more pizzazz than they can otherwise boast.

Combining tall, dark, and handsome:
Clematis 'Mikelite' (Viticella Group)
in *Cotinus coggygria* 'Royal Purple'.

Generally speaking, when planting clematis into established shrubs, keep the following in mind:

- Plant the clematis at the drip line of the shrub's canopy.
- When planting into acid-loving shrubs (rhododendrons, camellias), be sure to give the clematis its regular feed of organic rose and flower food, or surround (but do not cover) the crown with a generous handful of crushed oyster shells to slowly raise the pH.
- If the shrub has been limbed up like a small tree, a panel (12 to 24 inches/30 to 60 cm wide) of chicken wire or fencing cloth may be necessary to help the clematis leap into the shrub. Secure it behind the clematis with ground staples, and attach to a low branch of the shrub with Velcro tape.
- If the shrub is a water hog, make sure to water the clematis well and often during the first growing season after planting.

Autumn color is another factor that can work in your favor. Many clematis rebloom, so whether you're putting an herbaceous perennial in front of the shrub, growing a vine into it, or selecting a clematis as a backdrop, note whether the clematis can be made to rebloom, or will bloom late in the season, to add to an autumn vignette.

Clematis 'Countess of Lovelace' (Large-flowered Hybrid) in a rhododendron. Consider your options: do you want the clematis to bloom with the rhodie, or later, when the shrub is out of bloom? This clematis will do both, reblooming in the late summer, too.

Clematis in Conifers

Growing clematis in conifers takes more study. Some popular conifers, such as *Juniperus communis* 'Gold Cone', do not like having a clematis lolling all over them, and will go brown under the vine. This is disturbing in the late autumn or winter when the clematis is pruned and the conifer's discomfort is revealed. The brown patch will not recover until active growth starts again in the spring.

Other conifers, such as *Chamaecyparis* (Hinoki cypress) and most pines, don't seem to mind a clematis hitching a ride for the season, as long as they don't have to do the heavy lifting all year long. For conifers, consider lighter weight clematis vines, and those needing winter hard pruning.

When planting clematis into conifers, make sure the vine is planted at the drip line (outer edge) of the conifer's canopy. If the conifer is young but you know it will have a broad base eventually (such as *Cryptomeria japonica* 'Elegans'), it may look a little funny at first to be planting the clematis so far from the plant, but it pays to plan ahead. One can always make a temporary trellis for the clematis until the conifer's lower branches reach the vine.

The aforementioned cryptomeria has wonderful French puce foliage color through the winter and looks terrific with winter-flowering clematis planted into it, such as *Clematis cirrhosa* 'Ourika Valley' or *C. cirrhosa* var. *purpurascens* 'Freckles'. These clematis can get large, but if pruned to 3 feet (1 m) tall in June, they will grow enough to bloom well starting in November of the same year.

Explore the subtlety of picking up contrast with clematis stamen colors: *Clematis* 'Halina Noll' (Large-flowered Hybrid) in front of *Cedrus deodara* 'Snow Sprite'.

Clematis 'Polish Spirit' (Viticella Group) in *Chamaecyparis pisifera* 'Filifera Aurea'.

Clematis with Herbaceous Perennials

Perhaps clematis look so great with herbaceous perennials because some really good clematis *are* herbaceous perennials! Whether romping over a bank of autumn-blooming Michaelmas daisies (*Symphyotrichum*), forming an edging of flippy bells, or punctuating a repeated color rhythm, clematis blend well and readily whether they climb or are herbaceous perennials themselves.

One must always be careful that an excessively vigorous vine will not get too pushy with a tall willowy herbaceous perennial (such as *Helianthus ×multiflorus* 'Anemoniflorus Flore Pleno'), or that a short bushy clematis will not get buried by a floppy herbaceous perennial (*Monarda* 'Violet Queen'), but such controlling of unwanted competition is what contriving a successful herbaceous perennial garden is all about. These plants are in a pitched conflict against each other; we gardeners are merely the referees. That a garden looks like a place where fairies frolic drinking dew all day rather than a battlefield of spilled chlorophyll is to our credit.

Fighting fire with fire: *Clematis* 'Niobe' (Large-flowered Hybrid) with *Hibiscus* 'Robert Fleming'.

Clematis 'Polish Spirit' (Viticella Group) with Orienpet lilies.

When planting clematis amongst herbaceous perennials, rest assured: there are many good clematis for the partial shade border. Do not think just because you only have enough light for lady's mantle and astilbes that there may not be several fine shade-loving clematis to add to the mix, both interesting species and large-flowered hybrids. Conversely, there are many clematis that can take sun from the ground up. Most of these cannot be said to be drought tolerant, however, and they do need heat to ripen their woody vines to produce more flowers.

Another consideration: most clematis that *are* herbaceous perennials (not vines) require at least six hours of sun per day. The same can be said for certain horticultural groups, such as the Texensis Group.

Clematis 'Perle d'Azur' (Large-flowered Hybrid) adds its serene periwinkle blue to a quiet, shady corner.

Finally, when planting clematis amongst herbaceous perennials (whether the clematis is a vine or an herbaceous perennial in its own right), remember, clematis roots spread more down- than outward. It is easy for them to get swamped by shallow-rooted or rhizomatous herbaceous perennials, which will choke the clematis crown and prevent new shoots from emerging. (You thought I was kidding with those war metaphors?) Clematis crowns need to be well weeded.

Herbaceous perennial clematis can span the seasons: *Clematis* 'Miranda' (Integrifolia Group) with *Iris* 'Penny Lane'.

Later in the season, *Clematis* 'Miranda' enhances its new partner, an unknown seed dahlia.

Clematis for Containers

Raising a clematis in a container above ground decreases its winter hardiness by a full zone. For instance, if you are in zone 7 and want to grow the small-flowered shorter-growing 'Jenny' (Montana Group) in a container, you are effectively turning it into a zone 8 plant, and it may not survive, even though it would easily do so if planted in the ground.

Containers for clematis should be deeper than they are wide (at least 14 inches/35 cm) and have ample drainage holes. Soil blends meant for storage of woody nursery stock are preferable to peat moss–based potting soil. When peaty soil breaks down, it assumes the texture of wet chocolate cake, inhibiting root growth and oxygen exchange. Root and crown rot are sure to follow. When the soil loses texture, it is time to wash the roots, prune them if necessary, and repot with fresh soil.

To judge whether a clematis will thrive in a container, read the mature height listed on its tag. Any vine that stays at or below 8 feet (2.5 m) will be easy to maintain in a pot. You may need to pinch the tips to maintain bushiness, but this can be done at the same time the plant is deadheaded.

Clematis in containers may show yellowing leaves, indicating a lack of magnesium in the soil. Tomatoes often suffer from the same problem, so using organic tomato fertilizer that includes magnesium sulfate (Epsom salts) in the formula gives two benefits, supplying the extra magnesium and acting as a blossom booster. Follow the directions on the package for use on container plants.

Other than the truly tiny, such as 'Little Artist', most members of the Integrifolia Group are too floppy to look well in containers unless one is willing to spend a great amount of time tying each stem to a support, or employing a peony ring or other gadget to hold the stems up. The plants fall open, exposing the bare lower stems and crown. Hardly decorative . . .

Clematis 'Little Artist' (Integrifolia Group), shown with *Bidens* 'Bidi Compact', is no taller than a ballpoint pen.

For a big pot: *Clematis* 'Semu'
(Large-flowered Hybrid) with
Hydrangea paniculata 'Limelight'.

Large-flowered hybrids for containers

C. Alaina 'Evipo056' (pink)
C. 'Asao' (pink)
C. 'Andromeda' (white/red bar)
C. 'Barbara Jackman' (lavender/red bar)
C. Bijou 'Evipo030' (lavender)
C. 'Blue Eyes' (blue)
C. Fleuri 'Evipo042' (purple)
C. 'Fond Memories' (white/red outline)
C. 'Hoshi-no-flamenco' (red)
C. 'Innocent Glance' (pink, double)
C. Josephine 'Evijohill' (pink, double)
C. 'Julka' (purple)
C. 'King Edward VII' (lavender-
  stippled pink)

C. Kingsfisher 'Evipo037'
  (lavender-blue)
C. 'Louise Rowe' (blue, double)
C. 'Piilu' Little Duckling (pink/red bar)
C. 'Pinky' (pink/red bar)
C. Rebecca 'Evipo016' (red)
C. 'Rüütel' (red)
C. 'Semu' (purple)
C. 'Snow Queen' (white)
C. 'Solidarnosc' (red)
C. 'Tsuzuki' (white)

Small-flowered clematis for containers

MOST MEMBERS OF THE ATRAGENE GROUP will do well for several years; especially good forms are highlighted here.

C. 'Brunette' (Atragene Group)
C. 'Cecile' (Atragene Group)
C. 'Dark Dancer' (Atragene Group)
C. 'Helios' (Tangutica/Orientalis Group)
C. 'Jenny' (Montana Group)
C. koreana var. fragrans (Atragene
  Group)

C. 'Lunar Lass' (Evergreen Group)
C. 'Ruby' (Atragene Group)

Clematis with Clematis

Is there any higher goal a gardener can aspire to than to grow clematis as companions for each other? It hardly seems likely. For combining clematis well, you need only to remember the advice for growing them with shrubs: plant the clematis far enough apart to avoid root competition.

It is helpful but not always strictly necessary to combine clematis with like pruning needs. If a Viticella Group vine wanders its new growth into a large-flowered hybrid, there may not be a problem as long as the weight of both plants is borne by a non-living structure. Together, they might overcome a living shrub.

Herbaceous perennial clematis can be grown with just about any other type of clematis as long as they are given some sort of surrounding support to keep them from getting flattened.

Even the Montana Group clematis can be good companions if the weight of the big vine is carried by a fence—or similar built structure—and the smaller clematis is planted where the sprawling roots of the bigger vine will not interfere. The suggestions are endless!

Clematis 'Étoile Violette' with
C. 'Madame Julia Correvon'
(both in Viticella Group).

Consider both color and texture contrast in clematis combinations, as here with *Clematis* 'Bill MacKenzie' (Tangutica/Orientalis Group) and *C.* ×*diversifolia* 'Heather Herschell' (Integrifolia Group).

Clematis hirsutissima var. *scottii* is ideal for hypertufa troughs.

Growing clematis in troughs

GIVEN THE VARIETY OF GROWTH HABITS within the genus *Clematis*, it stands to reason that some species will be made happier in gardens by reproducing as best one can their habitat in the wild. To this end, many gardeners make their own hypertufa containers to mimic soil conditions preferred by clematis native to alpine and high pH conditions, and to guarantee the plants ample drainage in moist climates. The typical mix for homemade hypertufa is a 1:1:1 ratio of perlite, Portland cement, and ground coir fiber (a more sustainable substitute for peat moss). Mix well and add water until a clump in your fist holds together but does not drip when squeezed.

The following clematis prefer troughs in full sun for successful cultivation in gardens. The three evergreen hybrids, which are derived from New Zealand species, are non-climbing but will drape nicely.

C. ×*cartmanii* 'Joe' (Evergreen Group)
C. 'Early Sensation' (Evergreen Group)
C. *fremontii* (herbaceous perennial)
C. *fruticosa* 'Mongolian Gold' (deciduous shrub)
C. 'Lunar Lass' (Evergreen Group)
C. *hirsutissima* (herbaceous perennial)
C. *integrifolia* Mongolian Bells 'PSHarlan' (herbaceous perennial)

Clematis 'Duchess of Albany' (Texensis Group) with *C.* 'Prince Charles' (Viticella Group).

Sometimes it's just about making a pretty picture in your garden: *Clematis* 'Solidarnosc' (Large-flowered Hybrid) with *C.* 'Solina' (Viticella Group).

Clematis 'Étoile Rose' with *C.* 'Étoile Violette' (both in Viticella Group).

Clematis as Cut Flowers

In the Netherlands and Japan, clematis have long been used as cut flowers. Generally speaking, the Japanese have concentrated on the elegant urns and bells of the Viorna Group to decorate their tea ceremonies, each blossom expected to provide a noncontroversial topic of discussion, should conversation flag. In the United States, Chalk Hill Clematis in Healdsburg, California, was one of the earliest specialist clematis growers. Original farm manager Murray Rosen developed their unique planting and harvesting methods for both large- and small-flowered hybrids.

For home gardeners, there are a few tricks to know that will make cut clematis longer lasting. First, one can always simply cut and float the flowers (in water only, no floral preservative) on short stems. The broad surface area of large-flowered hybrids makes this an extremely easy proposition. If using in vases, cut as long a stem as possible, back into old wood (stems that have turned brown and are developing bark), when the flowers are just cracking open. Cutting into the mature stem ensures the vascular system is woody enough

Clematis recta 'Midnight Masquerade' (Flammula Group) with *C.* 'Rose-colored Glasses' (Integrifolia Group).

to transport water to the flowers well. You may end up with more stem length than you will ultimately need, but the stems can be shortened when they are arranged. Cut the clematis stems the day before you need them, and condition in cool deep water in a dark place (and if you have access to a floral cooler, so much the better).

Many books and articles suggest using alcohol when cutting clematis, but fail to explain the what, where, when, and how. Lucky for you, your author has done some informal research and can divulge the following: plant-based forms of alcohol (most commonly methyl [wood] and ethyl [grain] alcohols) make excellent floral preservative for long-stemmed clematis. From the time the clematis are conditioned and throughout their life in a vase, use alcohol at a rate of 2 tablespoons per quart or liter of water.

If you purchase these alcohols in a drugstore, a small proportion of acetone will have been added to deter the foolish from drinking the stuff. The acetone does not seem to affect the clematis one way or the other. In liquor stores one may buy nearly pure ethyl alcohol (in the United States, the brand Everclear is most common, alcohol by volume [ABV] 95% or 190 proof), and you will need only to deter teenagers. Clear liquors such as gin or vodka work, but because they have less than half the ABV of Everclear, you will need to use twice as much in a quart of water. Needless to say, do not be wasting Aviation gin on clematis. Give 'em the cheap stuff.

Proprietary floral preservative may be added to the 2 tablespoons of alcohol at a rate of 1 tablespoon per quart of water, but doesn't seem to be as beneficial as the alcohol by itself.

As with any other cut flowers, remove any foliage that would be under water during conditioning or after arranging, and recut the stems every other day.

A bowl of floating clematis with hosta leaves greets guests at Chanticleer. Do not use a floral preservative when floating clematis blossoms; it has a deleterious effect on the sepals.

UNDERSTANDING THE GENUS

Clematis have been grown in gardens for hundreds of years. In fact, the root of the word clematis, *klĕma*, is ancient Greek for a vine or climbing plant. (Hence, we say **clem**-a-tis, not cle-**ma**-tis.) The refinement of breeding techniques and spread of the various species from one continent to another via human expansion mirrors the increasing importance of the genus to the horticultural arts.

The earliest species recorded in Europe for decorative use were *Clematis integrifolia*, an herbaceous perennial native to central Europe and into Asia as far east as Lake Baikal, and *C. viticella* (virgin's bower), from southern Europe along the northern shores of the Mediterranean and the Middle East. Both are durable plants. There is some overlap in the native range, and we might presume the occurrence of naturally occurring hybrids. Both *C. integrifolia* and *C. viticella* came into cultivation during the reign of Queen Elizabeth I, and shortly thereafter, a double form of the latter, *C. viticella* 'Flore Pleno', appeared.

The Viticella Group are easy-care garden vines, each one strong-growing and free-flowering. The flowers are considered small, mainly broad down- or out-facing bells, usually likened to pagoda roofs with their four sepals forming corners, if one uses one's imagination. Within these deciduous hybrids the colors range from white (usually with dark stamens), pink, and rosy to true red (or very close to it), light blue, and most shades of purple. The prevailing wisdom is to reduce the vines in this group to 12 inches (30 cm) tall when they are dormant in the winter. This hard pruning encourages a mass of fresh shoots to burst from the crown in the spring, which is much to be desired since this group flowers on its new growth. The only reason not to hard prune *Clematis viticella* or its hybrids is if you want the plant to attain an imposing height.

Clematis 'Pamiat Serdsta' (Integrifolia Group) and *C.* 'Negritianka' (Large-flowered Hybrid).

The Integrifolia Group are entirely herbaceous perennials. This is by far the easiest group to cultivate, and once established the clumps can be very long-lived and even drought tolerant. In the wild, the color range includes white, several shades of purplish blue (the type color), and lavender shading to pink. The cultivars that are selections of the species average 12–24 inches (30–60 cm) in height. If deadheaded after their first flush of blossoms fade, the plants (like any good herbaceous perennial) will come back into bloom in 30–45 days. Two or even three waves of bloom are to be expected, depending on your climate. Once the plants have gone dormant, the spent top growth should be cut down to the ground. Plants grown from seed of the typical bloom form show little variation, but if growing the white or pink forms from seed, expect to get mostly blue.

In the 1830s the first known crosses of *Clematis integrifolia* and *C. viticella* were made, and it was then discovered that the gene that inhibits climbing is exceptionally dominant. So what does one get when one crosses a compact, free-flowering herbaceous perennial with a vigorous climbing vine? Answer: a big, floppy, non-clinging and very floriferous herbaceous perennial.

When you cross the vigorous climbing *Clematis viticella* with *C. integrifolia*, the result is a bigger, floppier non-climber, *C. ×diversifolia* 'Eriostemon' (Integrifolia Group).

Clematis that climb do so by wrapping their leaf stems (petioles) around anything they come into contact with that isn't too broad for them to embrace. *Clematis integrifolia* has sessile leaves—the leaves develop directly from the stems—meaning they have no petiole. Creating sensitive cells to wrap around the twigs of a neighboring shrub or the wire of a cyclone fence is simply not in their gene pool. Though some of the *viticella × integrifolia* hybrids have lobed leaves instead of plain ones, and even boast a bit of petiole, there is no ability to climb. Generally and informally, these hybrids are called the ×*diversifolia* group, but at your garden center you will see them lumped with Integrifolia Group plants. If you want this estimable group to grow up straight and true to their full 4–6 feet (1.2–1.8 m), you will need to tie them to an upright structure. For a more natural look, let them work their stems through nearby shrubs, and their large loose bell or flat flowers will pop into the sunshine to tell the most enchanting texture and color stories.

Again, because we have not changed the basically herbaceous nature of the "diversifolia crosses," they will want hard pruning once dormant. Do this anytime between early winter and early spring.

Meanwhile, in Japan, or Development of the Large-flowered Hybrids

Many fascinating clematis are native to the islands of Japan, but whether two of the founding large-flowered species, *Clematis patens* (pure white to pale lavender-blue) and *C. florida* (white with near-black stamens), are counted amongst them is open to vigorous debate and further study.

Some issues are best left to others to sort. The important thing to remember is that both *Clematis patens* and *C. florida* are exceptionally unstable. Although the typical sports of *C. florida* are well documented and usually sterile, *C. patens* is even more genetically factious. Because it has a wider range of color and a propensity to sport fertile double flowers, one is suddenly faced with a plethora of breeding options. Rumors of a yellow variant of *C. patens* have surfaced from time to time for many years; this mythical plant, known as the "Beijing patens," may be the parent behind the near-yellow large-flowered hybrids, all of which are fleetingly pale yellow when they open, turning to cream or white within a day or two.

Clematis patens 'Yukiokoshi', a named wild selection, is testament to the genetic instability that makes breeding the adventure it is.

Clematis 'Gipsy Queen' (Large-flowered Hybrid) can be pruned to flower early (May) or late (July).

The mutable *Clematis florida* was first brought into European cultivation in 1776 from Japan. It has long been presumed Japanese gardeners naturalized both *C. florida* and *C. patens* from China, but several Japanese botanists dispute this, claiming their populations are either part of the original native ranges, or that the Chinese took the plants from *them*, rather than vice versa. The prevailing modern view is that *C. florida* had been brought to Japan from China, specifically the wild populations in Hubei noted by E. H. ("Chinese") Wilson in the early 1900s. Oddly, despite their claim to the original large-flowered species, the Chinese never appeared to do much with them, horticulturally speaking, whereas by the 1830s, when both *C. florida* and *C. patens* were gracing European and English gardens, the Japanese were beginning their love affair with not just these but a variety of Asian species. The Japanese deemed *C. florida* and *C. patens* sacred, and large-flowered clematis became fixtures in their temple gardens.

In 1835 a double white sport of *Clematis florida*, now known as *C. florida* var. *florepleno* 'Plena', was brought into European trade as *C. f.* var. *plena* (it has now been found growing in the wild in China—*again*), and a year later, the second sport, a bicolor named after Philipp von Siebold, arrived in England via the Netherlands. Both the double white and bicolor sports were known in Japanese gardens much earlier, and presumably have Japanese names lost in the mists of time. Various double variants of *C. patens* were also taken to Europe, along with garden forms renamed after English horticulturalists, such as 'Standishii' and 'John Gould Veitch'.

Clematis florida var. *florida* 'Sieboldiana' and *C. f.* var. *flore-pleno* 'Plena' can mutate back and forth to each other. The eldest plant of 'Plena' owned by the Rogerson Clematis Garden (obtained in 2002 by a private gardener and donated to the clematis collection in 2007) has sported to 'Sieboldiana' numerous times. And while 'Plena' may set a few seeds, 'Sieboldiana' is known to be sterile.

In the 1850s, another highly influential large-flowered species, *Clematis lanuginosa*, arrived from China, where it had been discovered by Robert Fortune. It is shorter growing—though still a true climber—with furry stems and buds, and the flowers can be *huge*. It is easy to tell if a modern hybrid has "lanuginosa blood," as it will have proportionately bigger fuzzy buds, which have a distinct twist where the sepal points meet.

The presence of *Clematis florida*, *C. lanuginosa*, and *C. patens*, with the addition of the darker-colored genes of *C. viticella*, led to what we think of as the first golden age of large-flowered hybrid development, from the 1860s to the beginning of World War I. Gardeners have resisted the push by taxonomists to break the large-flowered hybrids into small groups reflecting which founding parent has the most influence. Instead, we have only two subgroups, the early large-flowered hybrids (flowering for the first time in a growing season in late April or May and into June) and the late large-flowered hybrids (those showing *C. viticella* influence by flowering first in late June and into July).

The one problem with sorting clematis by bloom time is that human activity—namely pruning, both the timing and severity—can make the early late and the late early. This is made abundantly clear by growing the famous 'Jackmanii', a *viticella* × *lanuginosa* cross, and its many progeny. The distinctions "late" and "early" were thoroughly muddied when 'Jackmanii' was crossed with *Clematis patens*, producing the exquisite 'Gipsy Queen', who performs like a trouper no matter when she is pruned.

Clematis 'Omoshiro' (Large-flowered Hybrid).

The most challenging clematis you'll ever lust after!

CLEMATIS FLORIDA VAR. FLORIDA 'SIEBOLDIANA' has a long and illustrious history of being famously difficult to grow. That it is child's play to propagate from cuttings makes the capricious nature of the mature plant all the more heartbreaking. This vine wants it all, and even provided with every luxury of cultivation, it may still decide to be shy with its blooms, take a year off from growing altogether, or simply flower like mad for a season before dying. And yet we want; we desire; we lust. Here is what you need to know and should try to do to make *C. florida* var. *florida* 'Sieboldiana' (and var. *flore-pleno* 'Plena') happy:

- Provide full sun from the ground up. Heat ripens the flowering stems.

- Provide regular water. These are *not* drought-tolerant plants.

- Provide free-draining soil. If grown in a container, add gravel—the less peat the better—and repot every other year.

- Use organic rose and flower food often. These plants are heavy feeders.

- This is going to kill you, but you *must* hard prune every year to 12 inches (30 cm) tall, in the winter. Mature growth is 5–10 feet (1.5–3 m) annually.

- Hardy in zones 6–9, but provide protection against drying, freezing winter winds, which are deadly.

Bon chance!

Clematis florida var. *florida* 'Sieboldiana'.

Clematis viorna lends its name to a large group of clematis with urn-, bonnet-, or bell-shaped flowers.

Enter the Americans

North America is the main home of a currently popular cadre of clematis, the Viorna Group. Two species, *Clematis fusca* and *C. ianthina*, both climbers, are native to China, Japan, and Korea; the rest of the vining viornae are scattered throughout the southeastern United States and up the Atlantic seaboard. Their nickname is the leather flowers, for their thick, tough-looking sepals and their urn-, bonnet-, or bell-shaped flowers. Call them what you will, these are plants of great subtlety and charm, and one of them, *C. texensis*, has had a tremendous influence on the large-flowered hybrids.

The French breeder Francisque Morel in particular, along with Lemoine et Fils of Lyon and the Jackmans in Woking, must have had very fine forms of *Clematis texensis*, which were used to great effect in the 1880s and 1890s to infuse true red into the blood of large-flowered hybrids. *Clematis texensis* is both an excellent stud and brood mare. It produces clouds of pollen, and its seeds are large and fecund. When it is the seed parent in a cross, the seedlings have flowers and cultivation requirements resembling their mother, with the lily-flowered tulip shape and vivid colors, usually pink or red. Within the Viorna Group, the hybrids whose mother is *C. texensis* (and who bear her the closest

East meets West: the two-tone bells of *Clematis versicolor* and the fuzzy dark flowers of *C. ianthina*.

resemblance) have their own designation, the Texensis Group. When *C. texensis* is the sperm donor, its color is inherited but not its shape.

As a clan, the Viorna Group, including the Asian species and the Texensis Group, should be treated like herbaceous vines, because that is what they are. Very little of the previous year's vine will rejuvenate, especially after a trying winter. Old stems may be removed (hard pruned) immediately after they go dormant. Abundant new growth will come from the underground crown the next spring. Typically the new shoots are reddish brown, so don't overlook them and assume the worst (they blend in especially well with clay soils).

The American vining viornae are undergoing a taxonomic revision. Expect to see perhaps as many as 20 new species burst onto the scene within the next few years, as well as clarification of a few native ranges and expected variability within some known species. A few of these species, previously known but undocumented, have already been given

The unassuming *Clematis reticulata* contributes the elegant straight-sided shape of its bell to its offspring.

Clematis texensis is the Holy Grail species for clematis collectors.

When *Clematis texensis* is used as a
pollen parent, it passes along its color
but not its form, as shown by C. 'Ville
de Lyon' (Large-flowered Hybrid).

their credentials. The newest to be recognized is *Clematis vinacea*, the first of the formerly mistaken clematis to earn a species designation in its own right. No other clematis behaves as it does, beginning its growing season giving the appearance of an herbaceous perennial, then starting to climb once it is bathed by midsummer rains in its native Tennessee.

The deceptively charming *Clematis* 'My Angel' (Tangutica/ Orientalis Group), a hybrid of *C. intricata*, is potentially invasive.

That about covers it for the history of the "glamour girls" of the genus, but there are several other small-flowered groups that bring their fascinating shapes, colors, and habits into our gardens.

The Tangutica/Orientalis Group

The small-flowered clematis producing yellow flowers do not, alas, intermarry with their large-flowered cousins. The Tangutica/Orientalis Group comprises species, including most notably *Clematis orientalis*, *C. tangutica*, and *C. tibetana*, that are mainly children of the steppes and high elevations in Asia, prepared for a life much harsher than the pampering they receive in a garden. We tend to treat them too kindly, and some of the species and their hybrids have ended up on noxious or invasive plant lists as a result. *Clematis intricata* is perhaps the worst offender if you garden in a temperate climate. Hard winters and lean soil make wild behavior less likely.

Clematis tangutica was first brought into cultivation in the late 1890s. It is distinct from its fellows in that the bright yellow lanterns have a rather straight-sided appearance, ending in points that flare out when the rest of the sepal does not. If you look at the profile of the buds from behind, they make a nearly perfect square. The sepals never flip completely wide, as those of *C. orientalis* do, and the buds are not spherical, as are those of *C. tibetana* and its vast array of natural varieties.

All species and cultivars in the Tangutica/Orientalis Group have showy seedheads, with silvery silken tails.

The bright yellow lanterns of *Clematis tangutica*, going to seed.

Clematis tibetana has a fascinating amalgam of characteristics, making for diverse garden uses.

The seeds of *Clematis mandshurica* progress from unripe green to mature dark brown.

The beauty of clematis seedheads

AS SEED-BEARING PLANTS GO, clematis are not particularly highly evolved. They have no containing structure for their seed (no ovary, for instance). Each ovum is housed in a pericarp (seed coat) that ends in a tail, either rudimentary (*Clematis viticella* has hardly any tail at all) or magnificent (the large-flowered species have curly golden tails that shine in the sun and look like a bouffant hairdo). *Clematis baldwinii* from the piney woods of Florida has straight tails up to 4 inches (10 cm) long, and *C. coactilis* has little cotton-topped white seedheads that look like so many little old ladies perched on the ridges of shale barrens. Many gardeners love the draping silver threads of the species in the Orientalis/Tangutica Group, which continue to blossom as the seeds of spent flowers develop.

In a few cases, the seed itself changes color as it matures, and the prettiest of these is *Clematis mandshurica*. Its autumnal hues offer a vast scope for harmonizing with flowering plants, and it is also quite natty combined with golden or light green conifers.

Many gardeners like to enjoy the seedheads of the large-flowered hybrids for a few weeks before deadheading and fertilizing to induce a second wave of bloom. Some large-flowered hybrids will rebloom well whether they are deadheaded or not, but by the time the next wave of flowers arrives, the seeds are looking tired as the plumy tails go dull and the heads shatter. Deadheading, or a simpler "clear cut" method of taking the whole plant down by half its height after its first bloom in May/June ensures any large-flowered hybrid will looks its best for its second bloom.

Besides *Clematis mandshurica* and any member of the Tangutica/Orientalis Group, the most attractive seedheads for garden use are *C. patens* and the hybrids 'Blue Ravine', 'Guernsey Cream', 'Peveril Pearl', and 'Toki'.

Big, Bold, and Beautiful: The Montana Group

For this group of clematis I devoutly wish we could install a perfume atomizer in each copy of this book, that the heavenly fragrance of Dan Hinkley's *Clematis montana* aff. *wilsonii* DJHC796 could waft over you as you read. Generally speaking, there is not a lot of floral color variance amongst the Montana Group, but they have other attributes, like their scent, that make them garden-worthy. Simply put, the flowers are pink or white, and double or not. Another oversimplification is to say they all get huge (to 40 feet/12 m), or that they all flower only in April and May, with *C. m.* var. *wilsonii* hort. carrying on a little later.

The Montana Group come from the Himalayas into China, notably Sichuan and Yunnan. Although *Clematis montana* first came into England in 1831, it was E. H. Wilson who brought its many natural variants and related species back from his tramps through China. Returning with him were *C. m.* var. *rubens*; *C. gracilifolia*, which flowers early

The evocatively fragrant *Clematis montana* var. *wilsonii* hort. is one of the most fragrant vines of the genus.

with pale pink flowers fading to white; and *C. spooneri*, which is unimpeachably white and often seen in the wild leaping into Lijiang spruce (*Picea likiangensis*) by using *Rosa sericea* subsp. *pteracantha* f. *omeiensis* as a step stool.

Wilson also brought back *Clematis montana* var. *wilsonii*, which promptly got confused in the trade, and what is sold as his variant is, in fact, nothing like what he described. That's why we add "hort." or "of hort." on plant tags; meaning that's the name we have agreed to use in horticulture for a particular plant, but what we sell is not the true thing according to Wilson's herbarium specimens.

Clematis chrysocoma, another closely allied Montana Group species, is the single most misunderstood plant in the entire genus, and that's saying something. The Latin epithet means "golden-haired," so any Montana Group form found growing where this should be is called by that name even if it has clear hairs that look gold only in certain lights. Never mind that *C. chrysocoma* is a non-climbing, short-stemmed shrub (no more than 2–4 feet/0.5–1.2 m). Although the plant has long been well known amongst modern plant explorers, only in recent years has the real deal crept without much fanfare into the trade, thanks to Dan Hinkley.

Many of the pink-flowering vines in this group are derived from *Clematis montana* var. *rubens* and have lovely red-bronze foliage. How well the leaf color holds through the growing season is variable, but the color is brilliant, with leaves emerging just after the vine starts blooming.

The slow-growing *Clematis* 'Freda' has the deepest pink of the Montana Group.

Evergreen clematis: growing *Clematis armandii* et al.

Clematis 'Hendersonii Rubra', an evergreen clematis collected in the wild by E. H. Wilson.

EVERYONE WANTS A FRAGRANT FLOWERING EVERGREEN VINE to grow by the front door, right? Be careful what you wish for, unless you never want to see your front door again. The most commonly available evergreen species is *Clematis armandii*, along with its selection 'Snowdrift' and the hybrid 'Apple Blossom'. These have glossy, dark green, vaguely scimitar-shaped leaves (although the foliage of 'Apple Blossom' may be more rounded), and where they are hardy (zone 7 and warmer) grow with great vigor to 40 feet (12 m) in length. The vines become heavy with age.

Clematis armandii is sought for both its four-season evergreen presence and its fragrant flowers, but it is something of a trick to grow. Consider these points:

- If the bottom 5–6 feet (1.5–1.8 m) of the plant are in the shade, or the vine comes to shade itself, the lower leaves will drop and not be replaced. This gives the base a "trunky" mature look you may or may not like.

- The flowers bloom only in March and April. If there is a hard late frost, the year's blossoms will be lost. Hence, siting this plant may be difficult even where hardy. Drying cold winds blacken the leaves even if the ground does not freeze. The dead leaves will not drop, or at least not as soon as you'd like.

- This clematis *must* be pruned or at least "thatched" every 2–3 years. The old leaves outlive their usefulness or become shaded by new growth. However, the vine is not quick to shed them, and the dead brown or black leaves create a heavy layer of thatch. Mildew may result.

- Provide a durable, sturdy structure. Do not *underestimate* how big this vine will get, and do not *overestimate* how many plants you will need to cover a desired area. This is not like cooking with garlic, where if one clove is good, two are better. One plant is usually sufficient to cover a vast swath of cyclone fence.

- *Clematis armandii* and other evergreen clematis are not good companion plants. Their leaves cut off light to any host plant, killing it by starvation. If planted into a large broadleaf evergreen, death will be by strangulation instead.

In summation, where it is hardy, this is the most widely misused species in the entire genus. And no, there are no purple hardy evergreen clematis. *Clematis armandii* does not mate with its cousins.

Clematis macropetala 'Maidwell Hall' is a prime example of the Atragene Group. Hard to imagine it being overlooked.

The Atragenes

The Atragenes—an ungainly name for a glorious group, perhaps the most underrated and underutilized horticultural group in *Clematis*. These are the hardiest of the hardy clematis, represented by species all the way around the Northern Hemisphere in the most difficult habitats, withstanding the deepest cold. The group includes *C. sibirica*. Need we say more?

Carl Linnaeus set this group apart from other clematis, giving its species their own genus, *Atragene*. Once absorbed into *Clematis*, the former name stuck around as the group name. It comes from Greek, and the final e is pronounced, as in the Greek names Penelope and Daphne, hence at-**rah**-jeh-knee. (Yes, other names for the group have been proposed, but none have stuck.)

Of the approximately 17 species in the group, the most commonly hybridized are *Clematis alpina* (the type species for the group), *C. koreana*, and *C. macropetala*. In temperate climates with enough winter cold to please them, most species and hybrids will rebloom at least once during the growing season after starting in March and April. Selections of *C. koreana* bloom nearly nonstop. The great Swedish clematis scholar Magnus Johnson used many of the lesser species in his breeding work, including *C. fauriei* from Japan and *C. ochotensis* from northeast Asia. The North American members of this group have never been used in commercial breeding, but for native plant lovers, a well-grown spread of *C. occidentalis* var. *grosseserrata* is no mean thing.

The distinguishing trait throughout the Atragene Group is the expanded ring of pet-aloid staminodes comprising the outermost whorl or two of stamens. These can be nar-rower versions of the four sepals—giving the *Clematis macropetala* cultivars their "ballet skirt" look—or shorter and somewhat spoonlike (spatulate) in the *C. alpina* selections such as *C. a.* 'Pamela Jackman'. The group is also notable for being largely composed of wood-landers who will tolerate partial shade or a northern aspect. *Clematis occidentalis* is one of few exceptions to the rule; it and its two varieties prefer a more exposed and sunny site.

Clematis alpina 'Pamela Jackman' (Atragene Group) makes up for being single by its depth of color and abundance of bloom.

Combining clematis groups is high art: *Clematis* 'Danuta' (Large-flowered Hybrid) from Poland and 'Fudo' (Viorna Group) from Japan.

There are several other clematis horticultural groups, and you will find the most outstanding species or hybrids from these lesser-known groups in the plant directory.

It can easily be claimed that we are enjoying a second golden age of clematis breeding, beginning in the late 1980s and escalating still today. Vivid colors arrive annually from Poland. Large-flowered clematis bred especially for container gardening come from England and Japan, and the Japanese are working wonders hybridizing within the Integrifolia and Viorna Groups. In Canada and the Netherlands, adding fragrance to the large-flowered hybrids is a focus, and also from the Dutch come innovative new vines in the Viticella and Texensis Groups. New Zealand sends us beautiful, durable clematis, and the genus continues to be a focus of study for plant explorers.

196 CLEMATIS FOR THE GARDEN

LARGE-FLOWERED HYBRIDS

Clematis Alaina
'Evipo056'

pink, single

Although a fairly new cultivar, this is fast establishing itself in the cut flower trade, and also as a garden favorite for the plump truly pink flowers. The flowers can be pointed to rounded, and the pink is a deep rose upon opening, softening to bubblegum pink with a darker midrib. This has been bred to flower on short growth but may get taller than the advertised height in optimal conditions with little pruning.

HEIGHT 3.5–5 feet (1–1.5 m)
LIGHT EXPOSURE Full sun to dappled or partial shade.

PRUNING Prune by one-half in late winter for early spring bloom. Deadhead after first flowering for best rebloom. Hard prune in winter in climates below zone 7.
BLOOM TIME First wave of blooms in late April through late May. Deadheading and fertilizing will produce more flowers in 30–45 days.
LANDSCAPE USE Shade tolerant; excellent in small shrubs; excellent in containers. Likely meant as an edge-of-the-border plant, but it gets a bit too tall for that use. Great in floribunda roses.
ZONES 4–9

Clematis 'Allanah'

red, single

From the garden of Allanah Edwards in Christchurch, New Zealand, to the world comes this rather gappy seedling, which in hot summer weather comes as near to true red as any large-flowered hybrid can. During a spring with cool nights, the color will drift toward burgundy. Autumn is the season when this cultivar offers its best. It is generally recommended that it be fairly hard pruned (by one-half to two-thirds its length) after the spring offering. In climates with hot summers, this may not be necessary.

HEIGHT 6.5–13 feet (2–4 m)
LIGHT EXPOSURE Full sun to afternoon-only light. Prefers hot sun to morning sun.

PRUNING Prune by one-half in late winter for early spring bloom. Deadhead by half the length after first flowering for best rebloom. Hard prune in winter in climates below zone 6.
BLOOM TIME First wave of blooms in early through late May. Deadheading and fertilizing will produce more flowers in approximately 45 days.
LANDSCAPE USE Shade tolerant but more free-flowering in full sun; excellent on trellises and rambling through tall hypericums with bold yellow flowers (such as *Hypericum forrestii*) or gold-foliaged shrubs. Also good against dark green, like a yew hedge.
ZONES 4–9

Clematis 'Andromeda'

white with red bar, single/semidouble

The self color of this starry beauty is white, which makes the deep pink-to-red blotch of color all the showier. This might have been placed with the stripy clematis—the brushstroke of cerise at the base of each sepal can hardly be called a bar—or it could have been lumped with the doubles, but in its double form, the power of that hint of color is blurred. Not that I mean to disparage this plant in any way, but I have been known to pick off the obviously double buds to encourage rapid formation of the single blossoms, which are much more charming. Needless to say, 'Andromeda' is an excellent rebloomer.

HEIGHT 6.5–13 feet (2–4 m)

LIGHT EXPOSURE Full sun to partial shade.

PRUNING Prune by one-half in late winter for early spring bloom. Deadhead after first flowering for best rebloom. Hard prune in winter in climates below zone 7.

BLOOM TIME First wave of blooms in late April through late May. Deadheading and fertilizing will produce more flowers in 30–45 days.

LANDSCAPE USE Against a dark yew hedge, the single flowers will shine like the stars they are. Great with roses such as 'Robin Hood' or 'Cerise Bouquet', where the rose is precisely the same color as the brushstroke on the white background. Excellent in containers.

ZONES 4–10

Clematis Arctic Queen 'Evitwo'

white, double

Many consider this the best double white clematis available, largely because it gets down to the business of blooming as a young plant more quickly than does 'Duchess of Edinburgh'. The blossom diameter is wider, too. Although some recommend it for containers, I have not found it to be particularly long-lived unless planted in the ground. This cultivar is double every time it blooms, but for the second flush to be as fully double as the spring display, don't be shy with the rose and flower food.

HEIGHT 7–8 feet (2–2.5 m)
LIGHT EXPOSURE Excellent in dappled or partial shade.
PRUNING Prune by one-half in late winter for early spring bloom. Deadhead after first flowering for best rebloom. Hard prune in winter in climates below zone 7.
BLOOM TIME First wave of blooms in mid-May. Deadheading and fertilizing will produce more flowers in 30–45 days.
LANDSCAPE USE Shade tolerant; excellent in small shrubs; excellent in containers short term.
ZONES 5–10

Clematis 'Asao'

pink, single

This clematis is often one of the earliest large-flowered hybrids to bloom, starting in mid-April and overlapping with the daphne, viburnum, and rhododendron seasons. The flowers are a bold, bright pink with lighter centers to the sepals, thus a display that can be seen for quite some distance. 'Asao' reblooms well in late August and is capable of throwing extra sepals during long cold springs. The reverse sepal surface has a green bar and is outlined with pink.

HEIGHT 7–10 feet (2–3 m)
LIGHT EXPOSURE Excellent in dappled or partial shade.
PRUNING Prune by one-half in late winter for early spring bloom. Deadhead after first flowering for best rebloom. Hard prune in winter in climates below zone 7.
BLOOM TIME First wave of blooms in mid- to late April through late May. Deadheading and fertilizing will produce more flowers in 30–45 days.
LANDSCAPE USE Shade tolerant; excellent in medium-sized shrubs; excellent in containers. The prettiest combination I've seen with this cultivar was a pairing with *Rhododendron* 'Cynthia'; the pink on dark pink is terrific, assuming one likes pink at all.
ZONES 4–9

Clematis 'Barbara Dibley'

pink with red bar, single

There is a case to be made for listing this vibrant cultivar amongst the ranks of red clematis, but as the flowers lose their first brilliance, the edges invariably lighten. In partial shade or in warm weather, the red bar is evident against the pink self from the beginning. Some might find this plant garish. The flowers are showy and broad, if a bit gappy. If you are fainthearted in matters of color, proceed at your own risk.

HEIGHT 6.5–10 feet (2–3 m)
LIGHT EXPOSURE Partial shade to full sun. This is surely the barred large-flowered hybrid most likely to resist sun-fading.
PRUNING Prune by one-half in late winter for early spring bloom. Deadhead after first flowering for best rebloom. Hard prune in winter in climates below zone 7.
BLOOM TIME First wave of blooms in late April through late May. Deadheading and fertilizing will produce more flowers in 30–45 days.
LANDSCAPE USE Likely to be lanky, so this vine is best used in dwarf conifers and other stalwart shrubs.
ZONES 4–10

Clematis 'Barbara Jackman'

lavender with red bar, single

The pictures on the labels of this cultivar do not do it justice; therefore it only ever sells when in bloom. The flowers are not large, but they are of a lovely shade of lavender with what could better be called a brushstroke of red rather than a bar. The red bar reaches only two-thirds of the way down the sepal, and the red is more stippled than it is a solid stripe of color. Thus, the red is not overwhelming, and the whole is surprisingly blendable with roses and other clematis.

HEIGHT 6.5–10 feet (2–3 m)
LIGHT EXPOSURE Excellent in dappled or partial shade.
PRUNING Prune by one-half in late winter for early spring bloom. Deadhead after first flowering for best rebloom. Hard prune in winter in climates below zone 7.
BLOOM TIME First wave of blooms in late April through late May. Deadheading and fertilizing will produce more flowers in 30–45 days.
LANDSCAPE USE Shade tolerant; excellent in small shrubs; does well in containers if tip growth is pinched to encourage bushiness.
ZONES 5–10

Clematis 'Beautiful Bride'

white, single

The best white large-flowered hybrid to come along in ages. The elegantly pointed sepals and subtle dark-anthered "eyes," in addition to the volume of bloom from the ground up, assure this cultivar a bright future. It is unusual to find a white clematis with anthers dark but filaments and pistils white, producing a smoky effect that makes this an ideal partner for dark-foliaged shrubs. The only trick with 'Beautiful Bride' is ensuring one doesn't overwhelm the host.

HEIGHT 7–9 feet (2–3 m)
LIGHT EXPOSURE Best in full sun, and especially effective in climates with a tendency to overcast conditions.

PRUNING Prune by one-half in late winter for early spring bloom. Deadhead after first flowering for best rebloom. Hard prune in winter in climates below zone 7.
BLOOM TIME First wave of blooms in May/June. Deadheading and fertilizing will produce more flowers in 30–45 days.
LANDSCAPE USE Terrific in dark-foliaged shrubs such as smokebush (*Cotinus* 'Grace' or *C. coggygria* 'Royal Purple'), purple-leaf Chinese witch hazel (*Loropetalum chinense* var. *rubrum*), or dark-leaf elderberry (*Sambucus nigra* f. *porphyrophylla* 'Eva' Black Lace). Also conforms well to shaped structures such as columns or tripod tuteurs. If given sun from the ground up, it will bloom from the ground up.
ZONES 4–9

Clematis 'Bees' Jubilee'

pink with red bar, single

This vine is named for the nursery that introduced it, Bees' Nursery. Although bumblebees seem to enjoy it, they had nothing to do with the bestowing of the cultivar name. The parentage here is undocumented, but the impression is one of softness. One can see 'Nelly Moser', but these flowers are plump rather than gappy. The self color is a creamy pink, and the bar is cerise with blended, rather than strident, edges into the pink.

HEIGHT 6–13 feet (1.8–4 m)
LIGHT EXPOSURE Excellent in dappled or partial shade.
PRUNING Prune by one-half in late winter for early spring bloom. Deadhead after first flowering for best rebloom. Hard prune in winter in climates below zone 7.
BLOOM TIME First wave of blooms in late April through late May. Deadheading and fertilizing will produce more flowers in 30–45 days.
LANDSCAPE USE Shade tolerant; capable of ranginess, this is an ideal cultivar for scrambling through rhododendrons or larger hydrangeas.
ZONES 5–10

Clematis Bijou 'Evipo030'

lavender, single

This plant was bred to be a cute little dickens, and it is. What other large-flowered hybrid can be used as an edging? The starry lavender flowers are not huge, but on this tiny plant they will cover the foliage with a dazzling display of color. While Bijou can climb, it usually turns its attention to flowering so quickly after bud break in the spring that it simply doesn't give itself the chance to gain any height.

HEIGHT up to 3 feet (1 m)
LIGHT EXPOSURE Full sun to dappled shade.
PRUNING Prune by one-half in late winter for early spring bloom. Deadhead after first flowering for best rebloom. Hard prune in winter in climates below zone 7.
BLOOM TIME First wave of blooms in late April through late May. Deadheading and fertilizing will produce more flowers in 30–45 days.
LANDSCAPE USE Shade tolerant; excellent as a repeated border edging; excellent in containers.
ZONES 6–9

Clematis 'Blue Eyes'

blue, single

Yes, blue is a relative term in the clematis world. This light blue clematis is, honest, bluer than most. The color is captivating, a lighter version of forget-me-not blue. The blossoms are of average diameter, but the sepals are pointed, giving a starry effect. Often the strong green bar on the reverse of the sepals will show through to the upper surface, adding another interesting detail to the whole.

HEIGHT 7–9 feet (2–3 m)

LIGHT EXPOSURE Excellent in dappled or partial shade.

PRUNING Prune by one-half in late winter for early spring bloom. Deadhead after first flowering for best rebloom. Hard prune in winter in climates below zone 7.

BLOOM TIME First wave of blooms in late April through late May. Deadheading and fertilizing will produce more flowers in 30–45 days.

LANDSCAPE USE Shade tolerant; excellent in small shrubs; great in containers.

ZONES 5–10

Clematis 'Blue Ravine'

lavender-blue, single

Granted, this clematis may be more lavender than blue, but it is one of the very best doers in partial shade. The large, slightly gappy flowers are abundantly produced and add a wonderfully smoky atmosphere to dappled corners. You could not do better for covering the bare lower legs of climbing roses or the bottom trunk of a Callery pear. In some climatic conditions there may be a faint pink bar.

HEIGHT 7–9 feet (2–3 m)

LIGHT EXPOSURE Excellent in dappled or partial shade.

PRUNING Prune by one-half in late winter for early spring bloom. Deadhead after first flowering for best rebloom, and if the vine is getting rangy, take off an extra 2–3 feet (0.5–1 m) at that time to maintain bushy foliage. Hard prune in winter in climates below zone 6.

BLOOM TIME First wave of blooms in late April through late May. Deadheading and fertilizing will produce more flowers in 30–45 days.

LANDSCAPE USE Shade tolerant; attractive seedheads. Excellent in shrubs, climbing roses, and small trees.

ZONES 5–10

Clematis Bourbon 'Evipo018'

red with pink bar, single

This is the classic raspberry red with a lighter pink bar. It is apparent from the coloration of this clematis that Raymond Evison was attempting an improved 'Ville de Lyon' with this cultivar. Whether or not you think he succeeded, Bourbon is a lovely flower in its own right. Being a lover of red clematis, I grow both. This new version has broader, more pointed sepals but is just as capable of rambling.

HEIGHT 5–6.5 feet (1.5–2 m)
LIGHT EXPOSURE Full sun to partial shade.
PRUNING Prune by one-half in late winter for early spring bloom. Deadhead after first flowering for best rebloom. Hard prune in winter in climates below zone 6.
BLOOM TIME First wave of blooms in late April through late May. Deadheading and fertilizing will produce more flowers in 30–45 days.
LANDSCAPE USE Sun or shade tolerant; excellent in roses, especially good in *Rosa* Double Delight 'Andeli', 'Leda', 'Hebe's Lip', and the like; bred for containers, but can get too lanky.
ZONES 4–9

Clematis 'Candida'
white, single

Want to make sport of your neighbors? Grow this unpruned into a deciduous magnolia. 'Candida' will bloom later than the small tree, and you may tell the gullible your magnolia reblooms—three times! This was the first large-flowered white clematis I bought for my garden, and it is still with me, 25 years later. There is a reason many antique clematis (1862 in this case) are still with us: they're darned good plants. This one is the result of a cross between *Clematis lanuginosa* and *C. patens*. The green bar on its reverse, inherited from *C. patens*, does not read through the top surface, leaving 'Candida' one of the whitest whites. If anything, the central bar is whiter than the edges! Pale stamens enhance the pristine appearance. The sepals are broad and well overlapped, rounded at the tips.

HEIGHT 8–15 feet (2.5–4.5 m)
LIGHT EXPOSURE Excellent in dappled or partial shade.
PRUNING Prune by one-half in late winter for early spring bloom. Deadhead or groom after first flowering for best rebloom, although if you leave it tall, it will rebloom anyway, just not as quickly. Hard prune in winter in climates below zone 7. In mild climates, if maximum height is required, prune only every third year in late winter. This gets those big white flowers well up into trees.
BLOOM TIME First wave of blooms in late April through late May. Fertilizing will produce more flowers in 30–45 days.
LANDSCAPE USE Shade tolerant; good for large shrubs and small trees; too rangy for containers.
ZONES 5–10

Clematis 'Candy Stripe'

lavender with red bar, single

These flowers are larger than those of 'Barbara Jackman', and have more of the courage of their convictions. When grown in partial shade with ample fertilizer, the lavender sepals are bisected boldly by the bright red bar. No running out of gas halfway down the sepals for these stripes. Fades badly when planted facing full west. The summer heat does these flowers no favors.

HEIGHT 7–10 feet (2–3 m)

LIGHT EXPOSURE Excellent in dappled or partial shade.

PRUNING Prune by one-half in late winter for early spring bloom. Deadhead after first flowering for best rebloom. Hard prune in winter in climates below zone 7.

BLOOM TIME First wave of blooms in late April through late May. Deadheading and fertilizing will produce more flowers in 30–45 days.

LANDSCAPE USE Shade tolerant; best used on a trellis or in medium to large shrubs such as arboreal hydrangeas and columnar dark conifers.

ZONES 5–10

Clematis 'Comtesse de Bouchaud' ✤

pink, single

Those who quibble over specific color words may object to saying this is pink. Early-season flowers may indeed have a lavender cast, but in warm weather there will be no doubt. This versatile vine may be pruned to flower at different times, performing solo or in partnership with companions. The flowers are not huge but are generously produced.

HEIGHT 7–12 feet (2–3.5 m)

LIGHT EXPOSURE Needs sun from the ground up to flower from the ground up.

PRUNING Prune by one-half in late winter for early spring bloom, or hard prune for a bountiful midsummer first bloom. Deadhead or groom after first flowering for best rebloom. Hard prune in winter in climates below zone 6.

BLOOM TIME First wave of blooms in late May. Deadheading and fertilizing will produce more flowers in 30–45 days.

LANDSCAPE USE This vine is the perfect choice for the wire fence at the back of a rose garden, making a lovely backdrop, or solo on an obelisk.

ZONES 4–10

Clematis 'Crimson King'

red, single

This cultivar has never been widely available in the United States, and one wonders why. It is a luscious crimson red, and generously free with its flowers. Although the height makes it lanky, it is perfect on an upright support towering over herbaceous perennials and dwarf shrubs. In Europe, this 1916 introduction is considered a classic.

HEIGHT 6.5–13 feet (2–4 m)

LIGHT EXPOSURE Excellent in any exposure.

PRUNING Either hard prune for summer bloom or prune by one-half in late winter for early spring bloom. Deadhead after first flowering for best rebloom. Hard prune in winter in climates below zone 6.

BLOOM TIME First wave of blooms starts in late May if pruned by half in winter. Starts flowering in late June if hard pruned then. Deadheading and fertilizing will produce more flowers in 45 days.

LANDSCAPE USE Too leggy for container culture, but terrific rambling through roses, or over the tops of out-of-bloom rhododendrons or camellias. The light yellow center blends well with creamy yellow flowers.

ZONES 5–10

Clematis 'Daniel Deronda'

purple-blue, single/semidouble

This vintage clematis is a rich lavender-blue, with sepals lighter in the center than at the margins. "Daniel" is capable of offering extra sepals in the spring, but not so many as to be welcomed amongst the truly double ranks. The lighter bar may, in certain light conditions, be seen as having a pink or peach cast. I thought the first person who said this was stretching one of my lower extremities until an innocent asked if the newly opened flower looked vaguely peachy along the midrib. And it did.

HEIGHT 7–10 feet (2–3 m)
LIGHT EXPOSURE Excellent in full sun to dappled or partial shade.

PRUNING Prune by one-half in late winter for early spring bloom. Deadhead after first flowering for best rebloom. Hard prune in winter in climates below zone 7.
BLOOM TIME First wave of blooms in late April through late May. Deadheading and fertilizing will produce more flowers in 30–45 days.
LANDSCAPE USE Shade tolerant; excellent in small to medium-sized shrubs, notably large shrub roses such as the peachy golden Jayne Austin 'Ausbreak'. Prune the clematis by as much or as little as you prune the rose to make life easier.
ZONES 4–10

Clematis 'Danuta'
pink, single

This is an excellent shade of slightly lavender pink from Brother Stefan Franczak of Poland. Although it can grow tall, it also makes a charming and bountiful groundcover in mid- to full sun. Even if given a small tree to climb into, 'Danuta' may decide to make a pink pool of itself upon the ground.

HEIGHT 7–9 feet (2–3 m)
LIGHT EXPOSURE Full sun or partial shade, but perhaps better in full sun, as the color does not fade.
PRUNING Prune by one-half in late winter for early spring bloom. Deadhead after first flowering for best rebloom. In climates with a long growing season, hard prune a second time in midsummer for a spectacular autumn show. Hard prune in winter in climates below zone 6.
BLOOM TIME First wave of blooms in late April through late May. Deadheading and fertilizing will produce more flowers in 45 days.
LANDSCAPE USE Shade tolerant; excellent in medium to large shrubs; makes an excellent groundcover, especially planted in pairs or groups of three.
ZONES 5–10

Clematis 'Doctor Ruppel'
pink with red bar, single

This cultivar is unique in being one of the only clematis selected or hybridized (we really don't know which) from South America. Early flowers look light pink with a strong dark pink bar—plays to the back of the house, as the theater people say—which changes over the life of each flower, adding mauve highlights. Flowers are bright pink with a red bar at maturity. These flowers have great presence, and there are often enough of them to obscure the foliage. Well-grown plants are unusually durable and long-lived.

HEIGHT 6–12 feet (1.8–3.5 m)
LIGHT EXPOSURE Excellent in dappled or partial shade, tolerates western exposures in coastal climates.
PRUNING Prune by one-half in late winter for early spring bloom. Deadhead after first flowering for best rebloom. Hard prune in winter in climates below zone 7.
BLOOM TIME First wave of blooms in late April through late May. Deadheading and fertilizing will produce more flowers in 30–45 days. I know of a 'Doctor Ruppel' in Garibaldi, Oregon, that has never had less than ten blooms on it throughout the summer and autumn.
LANDSCAPE USE Shade tolerant; give it a stout piece of trellis or a nice old rhododendron to decorate.
ZONES 5–10

Clematis 'Duchess of Edinburgh'

white, double

This cultivar makes a pompon of modest diameter but impressive depth. Blossoms have even been known to produce a short central stalk seemingly out of the boss of stamens with another enthusiastic whorl of sepals. Hybrids involving this "Duchess" have been known to do the same; just when you think the bud is fully opened, it telescopes out with another layer. Buds produced during cold spring weather will show a considerable amount of green in the outermost sepals, as well as an irregularity of shape. Indeed, a whole lower whorl of green bracts may form on the flower stem, increasing the effect of a blossom not quite ripened. Because this whole production can take such a long time to unfurl, you may as well sit back and enjoy the show. The autumn flowers will be whiter and more uniform, for those who are comforted by such things. Me? I rather like the misbehavior of spring.

HEIGHT 4.5–10 feet (1.5–3 m)

LIGHT EXPOSURE Needs full sun to produce the whitest flowers and to rebloom well.

PRUNING Prune by one-half in late winter for early spring bloom. Deadhead after first flowering for best rebloom. Hard prune in winter in climates below zone 7.

BLOOM TIME First wave of blooms in late April through late May. Deadheading and fertilizing will produce more flowers in 30–45 days.

LANDSCAPE USE This can be a rangy vine, best grown on an ample trellis or hosted by a large shrub.

ZONES 5–10

Clematis 'Edomurasaki' Blue Bird

purple, single

If you want a big showy deep purple clematis capable of blooming more or less all summer, you will look far to do better than this lovely hybrid. It makes a leggy plant and is therefore not the best choice for containers, but it has many other stellar garden uses. The list of possible shrub partners is nearly endless. I must take issue with the wholly unnecessary trade name affixed to this plant. The clematis oeuvre already has a perfectly good small-flowered hybrid of the Atragene Group named 'Bluebird' (one word). Using the name as a two-word trade name is simply duplicitous.

HEIGHT 8–10 feet (2.5–3 m)
LIGHT EXPOSURE Full sun or partial shade (northern exposures are fine).
PRUNING Prune by one-half in late winter for early spring bloom. Deadhead after first flowering for best rebloom. Hard prune in winter in climates below zone 6.
BLOOM TIME First wave of blooms in late April through late May, with bursts of repeat bloom throughout the summer. Deadheading and fertilizing will produce more flowers in 30–45 days.
LANDSCAPE USE Shade tolerant; excellent in gray and variegated shrubs and larger shrub roses. A few suggestions: *Hydrangea macrophylla* 'Lemon Wave'; *Viburnum tinus* 'Bewley's Variegated'; *Rosa* 'Paul's Lemon Pillar', *R.* 'Shropshire Lass'.
ZONES 5–10

Clematis 'Ernest Markham'

red, single

This champion clematis is to red clematis what old European roses are to red roses: truly dark cerise pink, not really red. That said, 'Ernest Markham' is lumped with the reds, and it fits better there than anywhere else. This color matches perfectly with such classic roses as 'Zéphirine Drouhin' and 'Madame Isaac Pereire' and, like them, is capable of blooming off and on all summer.

HEIGHT 8–16.5 feet (2.5–5 m)

LIGHT EXPOSURE Best in full sun, but tolerates partial shade.

PRUNING Prune any way you want. By half in late winter will produce large early flowers; hard pruning produces big flowers later. If you want it to reach its full height, prune only as often as needed to keep the plant looking fresh and productive.

BLOOM TIME First wave of blooms in late April through late May if partially pruned in winter. Deadheading and fertilizing will produce more flowers in 30–45 days.

LANDSCAPE USE Best in large shrubs and shrub roses. Also handsome in big pink-flowering shrubs, such as *Deutzia* ×*hybrida* 'Magicien'.

ZONES 4–10

Clematis 'Fair Rosamond'

beige, single

Although this might easily have been lumped with the white large-flowered hybrids, the color is more like beige, and it is rarely as white as advertised. But none of that matters, because the color isn't the reason for growing it. Rather, grow this because it is fragrant. 'Fair Rosamond' is the last surviving cultivar of a scented-clematis breeding program from the Jackmans in the 1870s. The fragrance reminds me of primroses; others say it has a buddleja-like honey scent.

HEIGHT 4–13 feet (1.2–4 m)
LIGHT EXPOSURE Excellent in dappled or partial shade, to preserve the odd color.
PRUNING Prune by one-half in late winter for early spring bloom. Deadhead after first flowering for best rebloom. Hard prune in winter in climates below zone 7.
BLOOM TIME First wave of blooms in late April through late May. Deadheading and fertilizing will produce more flowers in 30–45 days.
LANDSCAPE USE Shade tolerant and slow growing, so fertilize well to get it into bloom when young. Nice grown solo, as a specimen on a columnar structure close to a path.
ZONES 5–10

Clematis 'Fairy Blue' Crystal Fountain

lavender-blue, double

A dispute about the name of this plant persists, but it is not our place to settle the matter here. Japanese breeder Hiroshi Hayakawa named it 'Fairy Blue', and the legitimacy of any other name is unknown. Nonetheless, this is an attention-grabbing clematis. The flowers consist of an outer array of "normal-sized" sepals, with a proliferation of spiky staminode sepals (or sepaloid stamens, if you'd rather) that may be blue like the sepals but tend to chartreuse green in the very center. The outer sepals fall away, leaving the flower to age the petaloid stamens into a tuft of light blue points. (Ha! Yet another term for the same structures.) This is a sport of 'H. F. Young'. The rebloom in autumn when combined with Michaelmas daisies such as *Symphyotrichum novi-belgii* 'Little Carlow' or *S. n.* 'Lady in Blue' is delightful.

HEIGHT 4–7 feet (1.2–2 m)
LIGHT EXPOSURE Half day of sun or more.
PRUNING Prune by one-half in late winter for early spring bloom. Deadhead after first flowering for best rebloom. Hard prune in winter in climates below zone 7.
BLOOM TIME First wave of blooms in late April through late May. Deadheading and fertilizing will produce more flowers in 30–45 days.
LANDSCAPE USE Shade tolerant; excellent in small shrubs, especially those with golden foliage; excellent in containers.
ZONES 4–9

Clematis Fleuri 'Evipo042'

purple, single

There is a bevy of short-growing purple/violet clematis, and I could easily have selected 'Burma Star' from Barry Fretwell or 'Sano-no-murasaki' from Sano Asai. All are cut from the same cloth: short-growing, small but abundant flowers, ample rebloom. I select the Raymond Evison form simply because it is most likely to stay available. However, even growing these side by side, it is hard to tell them apart. If you want a purple clematis for a container, you can't do better than one of these three. Fleuri is perhaps more violet than purple in full sun, 'Burma Star' has broader sepals, and 'Sano-no-murasaki' is more velvety.

HEIGHT 3.5–5 feet (1–1.5 m); 'Burma Star' can allegedly get taller, but I have never seen it more than 4 feet (1.2 m) tall.
LIGHT EXPOSURE Full sun to partial shade.
PRUNING Prune by one-half in late winter for early spring bloom. Deadhead after first flowering for best rebloom. Hard prune in winter in climates below zone 6.
BLOOM TIME First wave of blooms in late April through late May. Deadheading and fertilizing will produce more flowers in 30–45 days.
LANDSCAPE USE Shade tolerant; excellent in small shrubs; excellent in containers.
ZONES 5–10

Clematis 'Fond Memories'
white with red outline, single

This white/cream clematis edged with a pencil line of deep burgundy-to-red marked the beginning of a continuing color trend in clematis breeding. This beauty shows its *Clematis florida* heritage in both the dark eyes and capricious behavior typical of that species and its sports. The 2004 introduction of this cultivar seemed to open the floodgates as similar, older cultivars bred in Japan reached the Western market. In all cultivars of this type, the outline often appears to run into the veins of the pale self color, more so in warm weather. Like many clematis with *C. florida* as a parent, growth may be generous or miserly, and sudden collapses are par for the course. Patience is rewarded with fabulously elegant flowers.

HEIGHT 7–8 feet (2–2.5 m)
LIGHT EXPOSURE Needs full sun from the ground up.
PRUNING Hard prune in the winter, or whenever the plant collapses, fertilize, and keep well watered. It will give you at least one thrilling display per year.
BLOOM TIME Assuming a winter hard prune, first blooms open in June. The plant may then bloom all summer, or rest during the heat and rebloom in September and October.
LANDSCAPE USE Best grown on a dark or blue-gray background (think *Chamaecyparis lawsoniana* 'Blue Surprise') or on a columnar structure as a soloist.
ZONES 7–10

Clematis 'Fujimusume'

blue, single

First, the translation of the name, "wisteria's daughter" or "girl under wisteria bloom," is lovely. Second, this cultivar has a surprisingly pleasant perfume when you cup the sepals around your nose. Third, and most important, this is the large-flowered hybrid that comes closest to being true periwinkle blue. If you put this on a display stand with pretenders such as 'General Sikorski', 'Will Goodwin', or 'Daniel Deronda', this cultivar will positively glow in comparison—an effect that may in part be attributed to the smooth surface and uniformity of color throughout the sepal.

HEIGHT 4–10 feet (1.2–3 m)
LIGHT EXPOSURE Full sun to dappled or partial shade.
PRUNING Prune by one-half in late winter for early spring bloom. Deadhead after first flowering for best rebloom. Hard prune in winter in climates below zone 7.
BLOOM TIME First wave of blooms in late April through late May. Deadheading and fertilizing will produce more flowers in 30–45 days.
LANDSCAPE USE Shade tolerant; excellent in small shrubs (hydrangeas, spireas), fabulous in the autumn with any colorful deciduous shrub; excellent in containers if new growth is pinched to encourage flowering on short stems.
ZONES 5–10

Clematis 'Frau Mikiko'

purple, single

The proud purple bowls of this vigorous vine are as charming and handsome as the woman they were named for, Mikiko Sugimoto, wife of breeder Kozo Sugimoto. However, unlike its namesake, the vine is a bit sprawling and should be planted amongst shrubs to make its own pleasing effects. This clematis also produces some floriferous low lateral growth and would also serve well as a groundcover.

HEIGHT 8–10 feet (2.5–3 m)
LIGHT EXPOSURE Full sun or partial shade.
PRUNING Prune by one-half in late winter for early spring bloom. Deadhead after first flowering for best rebloom. Hard prune in winter in climates below zone 6. May occasionally be hard pruned in midsummer to keep the plant more compact.
BLOOM TIME First wave of blooms in late April through late May. Deadheading and fertilizing will produce more flowers in 30–45 days. Bloom can be nearly continuous throughout the growing season in fertile soil and full sun.
LANDSCAPE USE Best in a mixed border of shrubs and shrub roses. Flowers early enough to consort well with the once-blooming old garden roses. The vibrant purple color pairs well with autumn foliage. Who says purple isn't an autumn color? Also effective grown as a column.
ZONES 5–10

Clematis 'General Sikorski'

lavender-blue, single

The flowers of this Polish cultivar seem quite deeply lavender when they first open, and within just a day or two, the color shifts to something closer to blue. This vine is quite durable, suffering drought and deluge alike once well established. A trick to make this clematis seem bluer is to grow it with red or coral roses (or other flowers), which will complement the blue tones in the clematis blossoms.

HEIGHT 6–10 feet (1.8–3 m)

LIGHT EXPOSURE Bluer in full sun, but also excellent in dappled or partial shade.

PRUNING Prune by one-half in late winter for early spring bloom. Deadhead after first flowering for best rebloom. Hard prune in winter in climates below zone 7. When grown in roses, prune as you would the rose, and at the same time.

BLOOM TIME First wave of blooms in late April through late May. Deadheading and fertilizing will produce more flowers in 30–45 days.

LANDSCAPE USE Shade tolerant; excellent in roses and other medium to large shrubs; also makes a handsome specimen on a tuteur.

ZONES 4–9

Clematis 'Gillian Blades'

white, single

New blossoms of 'Gillian Blades' often exhibit a light lavender outline, especially in the spring bloom cycle when the nights are cool as the buds form. Given that the sepals have a pronounced "pie-crust" edging, to have this detail highlighted by soft lavender shadowing makes for a very pretty display. Within a day or two of opening, the flowers turn white, but the frilly edge makes a wall or column of 'Gillian Blades' quite a lively affair. This cultivar, named for one of clematis breeder Jim Fisk's secretaries, has the distinction of being the most durable clematis in my garden. An invasion of Himalayan blackberry necessitated the removal of 'Gillian Blades'. . . or so I thought. A year later, a root mass unseen in the soil debris sprouted a shoot and feebly bloomed. A year after that, new vines (clematis, not blackberry!) emerged from the site of the original plant.

HEIGHT 6.5–9 feet (2–3 m)
LIGHT EXPOSURE Sun to partial shade.
PRUNING In late winter, groom by a third, or hard prune.
BLOOM TIME May into June, with September rebloom.
LANDSCAPE USE Shade tolerant; in partial shade this will be rangy but still capable of lovely effects. Even in full sun, consider pinching the early tip growth to maintain bushiness, especially in containers. In full sun from the ground up, the lower stems will stay leafy if sufficiently watered, into midsummer.
ZONES 4–11

Clematis 'Guernsey Cream'

white, single

This clematis bears the most evocative name of any plant I know. Close your eyes, imagine what cream from Guernsey cows might look like, open them, and there's 'Guernsey Cream'. In this case, we also have a reference to the isle of Guernsey, home of its breeder, Raymond Evison. The flowers are not huge, but the sepals are rounded and pleasingly plump. This vine is capable of blooming in such profusion as to obscure the foliage entirely. One word of warning: like many of the near-white clematis having a hint of yellow in the newly opened blossoms (if you squint and hope), every single bruise from even the tiniest hailstone will show after a spring storm. The truly white clematis seem to have a stronger surface cuticle than the near-whites and rarely show as much damage.

HEIGHT 7–9 feet (2–3 m)

LIGHT EXPOSURE Best in full sun, but tolerates partial shade.

PRUNING Prune by one-half in late winter for early spring bloom. Deadhead after first flowering for best rebloom. Hard prune in winter in climates below zone 7.

BLOOM TIME One of the earliest, with first flood of blooms mid- to late April through mid-May. Deadheading and fertilizing will produce more flowers in 30–45 days.

LANDSCAPE USE The vigor of growth makes this hard to control in a container. Best used as a column, or on a tripod structure in the landscape. Ideal for covering the bare legs of climbing roses. Attractive seedheads.

ZONES 4–9

Clematis 'Hagley Hybrid' Pink Chiffon

pink, single

This vigorous and versatile hybrid has been done a disservice by having a trade name slapped on it over 50 years after being introduced. I have actually had someone say to me, "I never liked 'Hagley Hybrid', but I bought that new Pink Chiffon and I love it." It puts a person in a moral bind, that kind of thing. Then there are those who say 'Hagley Hybrid' isn't pink but rather lavender, further testing one's character.

HEIGHT 7–10 feet (2–3 m)

LIGHT EXPOSURE Flowers well in sun but fades after 2–3 days; excellent in dappled or partial shade.

PRUNING Prune by one-half in late winter for early spring bloom, or hard prune in late winter for first bloom in June/July. Deadhead after first flowering for best rebloom. Hard prune in winter in climates below zone 6.

BLOOM TIME Dependent on when pruning occurs. Deadheading and fertilizing will produce more flowers in 30–45 days.

LANDSCAPE USE Shade tolerant; excellent in small shrubs, especially the lower legs of climbing roses. Very pretty in *Abelia* ×*grandiflora*, especially since both flower best from late summer until frost; excellent in containers.

ZONES 4–9

Clematis 'Hakuokan'

purple, single

The translation of the name from Japanese, "white royal crown," gives one a good idea of the singular feature of this distinctive purple clematis: its brilliantly white to creamy boss of stamens. The flowers are not huge but are showy nonetheless. This cultivar will occasionally be seen as 'Hakuookan'; the extra o is added when using a more cumbersome transliteration method for converting Japanese symbols into written English. More modern versions do not require the double o to represent the sound "oh."

HEIGHT 7–12 feet (2–3.5 m)

LIGHT EXPOSURE Excellent in dappled or partial shade; fades slightly in full sun.

PRUNING Prune by one-half in late winter for early spring bloom. Deadhead after first flowering for best rebloom. Hard prune in winter in climates below zone 6.

BLOOM TIME First wave of blooms in late April through late May. Deadheading and fertilizing will produce more flowers in 30–45 days.

LANDSCAPE USE Shade tolerant; excellent in small shrubs; excellent in containers.

ZONES 4–9

Clematis 'Hayate'

purple, single

It was love at first sight of this 2008 introduction from Japan, for me. Others may call this wine-red, but the blossoms I've seen are far too violet for any wine I've ever consumed, especially when buds form in early spring with cold nights. The sepal surface has an irresistible satin sheen, and the overall shape is starry.

HEIGHT 6–7 feet (1.8–2 m)

LIGHT EXPOSURE Color holds well in full sun, but also excellent in dappled or partial shade.

PRUNING Prune by one-half in late winter for early spring bloom. Deadhead after first flowering for best rebloom. Hard prune in winter in climates below zone 6.

BLOOM TIME First wave of blooms in late April through late May. Deadheading and fertilizing will produce more flowers in 30–45 days.

LANDSCAPE USE Shade tolerant; excellent in small shrubs; excellent in containers. Lovely flowering in the smaller *Spiraea japonica* cultivars and romping through the ubiquitous *Euonymus fortunei* 'Emerald Gaiety'.

ZONES 5–10

Clematis 'Henryi'

white, single

This vintage (1870) cultivar is the classic choice for those wanting a durable white clematis for the light post at the driveway entrance, or to swath the mailbox. It is one of the biggest whites, both in the mature size of the plant, and the diameter of the flowers. Dark anthers add some interest at the center without looking spidery or overly "made-up." In the United States, 'Henryi' does much better where spring arrives quick and hot. In coastal regions, it can actually be hard to establish and will want plenty of sun to produce the volume of bloom that comes so easily in the prairie states.

HEIGHT 9–15 feet (3–4.5 m)

LIGHT EXPOSURE Flowers best in full sun, especially in coastal areas and climates prone to overcast.

PRUNING Prune by one-half in late winter for early spring bloom. Deadhead after first flowering for best rebloom. Hard prune in winter in climates below zone 7.

BLOOM TIME First wave of blooms in early April through late June. Deadheading and fertilizing will produce more flowers in 30–45 days.

LANDSCAPE USE Showy on built structures, and good in large shrubs needing summer interest, such as winter-flowering viburnums.

ZONES 4–10

Clematis 'Honora'

plum, single

Is it red? Not really. Is it violet? Perhaps, but not exactly. The RHS color swatches for this plant mention plum and garnet, so hopefully you get the idea—dark and dramatic. This selection comes from the same Christchurch, New Zealand, garden as the brilliant red 'Allanah'. Like 'Allanah', 'Honora' was taken to the astute clematis breeder Alister Keay, who introduced it. In any case, the plum-magenta color is yummy and fun to play with in plant combinations.

HEIGHT 10–13 feet (3–4 m)
LIGHT EXPOSURE Excellent in dappled or partial shade; fades a bit in full sun.
PRUNING Hard prune in late winter for a later spring start, or prune by half to begin flowering in May. Hard prune in winter in climates below zone 6.
BLOOM TIME First wave of blooms in late April through late May with a half-prune. This cultivar can have a wonderfully long season, as just when you think it is fizzling out, a branch will drape another meter-long arm of bloom around the shoulders of a tall shrub.
LANDSCAPE USE Shade tolerant; excellent in evergreen hedges or over arbors and pergolas.
ZONES 5–10

Clematis 'Hoshi-no-flamenco'

red, single

The truly red 'Gravetye Beauty' was one parent of this Japanese cultivar, bequeathing this plant its delicious shadings. The other parent, *Clematis patens* 'Manshuu Ki', provides the plump shapeliness. The sepals are broad and slightly rounded at the tips. The color is a rich shade of very deep pink (full disclosure: not truly red). The word "flamenco" in the name, just as you'd suspect, is a reference to the vibrant costume of a flamenco dancer.

HEIGHT 5–7 feet (1.5–2 m)
LIGHT EXPOSURE Either full sun or northern exposure. Color deeper in full sun.
PRUNING Prune by one-half in late winter for early spring bloom. Deadhead after first flowering for best rebloom. Hard prune in winter in climates below zone 7.
BLOOM TIME First wave of blooms in late April through late May. Deadheading and fertilizing will produce more flowers in 30–45 days.
LANDSCAPE USE Shade tolerant; excellent in small shrubs; excellent in containers.
ZONES 5–10

Clematis Hyde Hall 'Evipo009'

white, single

Many consider this cultivar Raymond Evison's best white. In cool weather the earliest flowers may have a pink cast, emphasized by the pinkish brown anthers. Like other whites from *Clematis patens*, it has the green bar on the reverse, which also has an influence on the relative whiteness of the sepals. There is also a gentle ruffle to the sepal edges, further enlivening the blossoms. This is one of the four outstanding clematis Evison introduced in 2004 to commemorate the 200th anniversary of the Royal Horticultural Society; each is named for one of the RHS gardens.

HEIGHT 7–10 feet (2–3 m)
LIGHT EXPOSURE Partial shade or full sun.
PRUNING Prune by one-half in late winter for early spring bloom. Deadhead after first flowering for best rebloom. Hard prune in winter in climates below zone 7.
BLOOM TIME First wave of blooms in late April through late May. Deadheading and fertilizing will produce more flowers in 30–45 days.
LANDSCAPE USE Shade tolerant; excellent in small shrubs; not long-lived in containers.
ZONES 4–9

Clematis 'Innocent Glance'

pink, double

The name of this swoon-worthy double was nearly lost in translation. Its Polish breeder, Szczepan Marczynski, planned to name it "innocent stare" until it was pointed out to him by a native English speaker (well American, anyway) that a stare is rude and a glance is flirty. And this flower is long on flirty. The generous petaloid sepals make for a lush spectacle, the color is a winning pink, and the bloom begins with sepals and petaloid sepals outlined in darker pink. The combination is dynamite. Blooms on new wood may be single or semidouble, but in a warm year with plenty of fertilizer, semidouble will be the norm. This clematis is worth viewing intimately, so place near a pathway.

HEIGHT 4.5–7 feet (1.5–2 m)
LIGHT EXPOSURE Needs full sun to produce the fullest flowers and to rebloom well.
PRUNING Prune by one-half in late winter for early spring bloom. Deadhead after first flowering for best rebloom. Hard prune in winter in climates below zone 7.
BLOOM TIME First wave of blooms in mid-May through late June. Deadheading and fertilizing will produce more flowers in 30–45 days.
LANDSCAPE USE Such a distinctive flower runs the risk of upstaging most host plants, even though the vine is not large and heavy. It is ideal for growing in a container for a few years. If using in a shrub, choose something that won't compete with the blossom time, and a white variegation wouldn't come amiss.
ZONES 5–10

Clematis 'Iubileinyi-70'

purple, single

This late-flowering clematis (aka 'Julileinyi-70', 'Jubilee-70') is exceptionally vigorous and rugged. The color is more violet than purple, attesting to 'Jackmanii' as a parent. The new canes burst from the ground in every direction, making this a good knitter of shrubs and also a perfect groundcover candidate. However, do not let it swamp its host plants! This is one of the best introductions from the largely unknown clematis breeding program in Ukraine during the Cold War. When the Berlin Wall came down, clematis came tumbling out!

HEIGHT 10–13 feet (3–4 m)
LIGHT EXPOSURE Best in full or at least afternoon sun.
PRUNING Hard prune in the winter.
BLOOM TIME First wave of blooms in early June. Pruning by half and fertilizing will produce more flowers in 45 days for a good autumn display.
LANDSCAPE USE Excellent in large roses (such as Jayne Austin 'Ausbreak' or 'Darlow's Enigma') and later-flowering shrubs such as *Sambucus nigra* f. *porphyrophylla* 'Eva' Black Lace or *Vitex agnus-castus*.
ZONES 4–10

Clematis 'Jackmanii'

purple, single

What else is there to say about this highly esteemed grandpappy of so many great large-flowered hybrids? The flowers are abundant. The color is compelling. The growth is always robust. In long-season climates, it is easily capable of three blossom cycles per year. What might be somewhat unknown is that if you do not hard prune in the winter, instead taking off only half the length, it will start flowering earlier (in May), and the flowers will be quite large. There is a reason we've all been growing this since 1863. Some modern plantsmen have said the original form is lost; but retired nurseryman Chris Sanders, who has clapped eyes on the Jackmans' original herbarium samples and description, reports that we are, largely, still growing the true thing. This is one of the four founding cultivars of the Rogerson Clematis Collection, originally purchased by Brewster Rogerson in 1971.

HEIGHT 10–13.5 feet (3–4 m)
LIGHT EXPOSURE Full sun.
PRUNING Normal practice is to hard prune in late winter for June/July flowers, but one can prune by one-half in late winter for early spring bloom.
BLOOM TIME First wave of blooms in mid- to late May if half pruned. Deadheading and fertilizing will produce more flowers in 45 days. In this case, these tasks may not be necessary.
LANDSCAPE USE Great on porches, arbors, and built structures. Also fine for decorating large spring-flowering trees (such as the cultivars of *Pyrus calleryana*) for later season color.
ZONES 4–10

Clematis Jackmanii Purpurea 'Zojapur'

purple, single

Once upon a time, say 125 years ago, the name "Jackmanii" was strewn about pretty liberally. With the true 'Jackmanii' established so firmly in the trade, people tacked the name onto just about anything else to attract attention. The modern breeder of the vine we're discussing here, Wim Snoeijer, maintains the true 'Jackmanii' has been lost (see 'Jackmanii' entry) and may have been trying to reproduce it in this cultivar. While I don't believe Wim is correct in his suppositions, I will readily admit this new cultivar is a cracking good plant. The flowers, while not large, are of a particularly carrying shade of violet with a lighter bar.

HEIGHT 7–9 feet (2–3 m)
LIGHT EXPOSURE Best in full sun.
PRUNING Hard prune in winter, then prune by half or more after the first flowering for a second late summer bonanza.
BLOOM TIME First wave of blooms in late May, more likely June. Deadheading and fertilizing will produce more flowers in 45 days.
LANDSCAPE USE Wonderful as a statement plant, as a column, or covering a flat-panel trellis.
ZONES 5–9

Clematis 'Jan Pawel II'

beige, single

'Jan Pawel II' (aka 'John Paul II') is another clematis producing flowers one might describe as beige. Officially this is described as creamy with a touch of pink. Sounds like beige to me, and having grown it, it looks that way, too, especially in partial shade. A slightly darker pink bar may be seen in blossoms tending to the shady side of the vine. Beige is hardly a color one would attribute to a pope who was so vigorously athletic in his early years. But the vigor of this clematis? It is formidable.

HEIGHT 7–18 feet (2–5.5 m)
LIGHT EXPOSURE Excellent in dappled or partial shade.
PRUNING Hard prune in late winter for bountiful late June/July flowering. Then prune by one-half for autumn rebloom. If you want this to get tall and stay tall, limit pruning to every third year.
BLOOM TIME First wave of blooms in late May through early July. Half pruning and fertilizing will produce more flowers in 60 days.
LANDSCAPE USE Shade tolerant; grows well in sun but the subtle color goes white quickly. Very free-flowering on lanky stems, so give it a mature deciduous tree to decorate, or sturdy arbor.
ZONES 4–9

Clematis Josephine 'Evijohill'

pink, double

This double was introduced by Raymond Evison but started life as a chance seedling purchased by Josephine Hill and sent to him for evaluation. It is likely a "cutting sport." The flowers are pink but variable. Typically large sepals open cotton-candy pink (candy floss to the British) and may or may not have a darker pink bar. The plethora of petaloid stamens most always have a bar, but occasionally these will be narrow and not especially well filled out. Weather seems to play a large role in the relative beauty of this flower. The outer sepals can go brown before they fall, and the remaining center can be a lovely puff of pink-cream or a dull spiky tan-pink. Nonetheless, many consider this the best pink double available.

HEIGHT 7–8.5 feet (2–2.5 m)
LIGHT EXPOSURE Needs full sun to produce the strongest colors and to rebloom well.
PRUNING Prune by one-half in late winter for early spring bloom. Deadhead after first flowering for best rebloom. Hard prune in winter in climates below zone 7.
BLOOM TIME First wave of blooms in early May through mid-June. The length of time it takes the flowers to fully open extends the bloom season. Deadheading and fertilizing will produce more flowers in about 60 days.
LANDSCAPE USE Most often seen growing in a container, blooming from the ground (on short stems) up.
ZONES 4–10

Clematis 'Julka'

purple, single

That this plant has 'Mrs. N. Thompson' as a parent comes as no surprise, given the depth and velvetiness of its purple color. 'Julka', however, does not have so obvious a red bar, and often only a hint of red highlights the midrib. The unique characteristic of this vine is the enthusiasm with which it blooms in the autumn, without much prompting. The color is better and the blossoms far more prolific on the current season's growth after a hot summer to ripen the wood.

HEIGHT 7–9 feet (2–3 m)

LIGHT EXPOSURE Color holds well in full sun. The color is perhaps too dark to show well in partial shade and would need careful placement.

PRUNING Prune by one-half in late winter for early spring bloom. Deadhead after first flowering for best rebloom. Hard prune in winter in climates below zone 7.

BLOOM TIME First wave of blooms in late April through late May. Deadheading and fertilizing will produce more flowers in 30–45 days.

LANDSCAPE USE Excellent in small shrubs; excellent in containers.

ZONES 5–10

Clematis 'Kacper'

purple, single

This flower is nothing short of grand. The color is truly violet, the surface is lush, and the diameter impressive. Many are the years this will produce the biggest clematis blossoms in your garden, with 10 inches (25 cm) not being at all uncommon. As if the stunning flowers were not enough, 'Kacper' can bloom in as many as three long-lasting waves in growing seasons longer than 110 days. This is rapidly becoming a favorite of the Franczak/Poland introductions. It's hard to overlook a plant that works so diligently to please.

HEIGHT 6.5–8 feet (2–2.5 m)

LIGHT EXPOSURE Full sun or partial shade.

PRUNING Prune by one-half in late winter for early spring bloom. Deadhead after first flowering for best rebloom. Hard prune in winter in climates below zone 7.

BLOOM TIME First wave of blooms in late April through late May. Deadheading and fertilizing will produce more flowers in 45 days.

LANDSCAPE USE Makes a wonderful show in variegated shrubs and complementary-colored roses, and will cover the ground if no vertical temptation is provided.

ZONES 4–10

Clematis 'Kardynal Wyszynski'

cerise, single

This cultivar is often lumped with the reds, but honestly, if this isn't cerise, well . . . what is? Its color is sometimes said to be carmine. If you look up "carmine," a dictionary will say "crimson." And crimson? "Any of several deep purplish reds," says *Merriam-Webster*. This might all be a clever ploy by the author to get yet another red clematis mentioned here. Heh heh. Be that as it may, this is a bold plant, vigorous and sturdy, boasting two long periods of bloom. In my garden it grows through *Rosa ×odorata* 'Mutabilis', where the clematis is the same shade as the final color of the rose petals before they fall. I'd suggest you do the same.

HEIGHT to 9 feet (3 m)

LIGHT EXPOSURE Full sun to partial shade.

PRUNING Prune by one-half in late winter for early spring bloom. Deadhead after first flowering for best rebloom. If grown in a rose, prune to the same degree you prune the rose, at the same time of year. Hard prune in winter in climates below zone 6.

BLOOM TIME First wave of blooms in early May through mid-June. Deadheading and fertilizing will produce more flowers in 30–45 days.

LANDSCAPE USE Shade tolerant; excellent in roses; too rangy for containers.

ZONES 4–10

Clematis 'King Edward VII'

pink stippled with lavender, single

The coloration of this clematis is so unusual that once you are familiar with it, you will never mistake it for any other. Imagine an otherwise nondescript pale pink clematis heavily stippled, or perhaps sponge-painted, with lavender-violet. The flowers look as though they've just escaped from a Seurat. The pointillist effect is unique. This clematis has a wide range of landscape uses and is an excellent rebloomer. Add to that its parentage, which blows my mind. You can look at one parent elsewhere in this book, 'Sir Trevor Lawrence'. Surprising.

HEIGHT 5–10 feet (1.5–3 m)
LIGHT EXPOSURE Excellent in dappled or partial shade.
PRUNING Prune by one-half in late winter for early spring bloom. Deadhead after first flowering for best rebloom. Hard prune in winter in climates below zone 7.
BLOOM TIME First wave of blooms in late April through late May. Deadheading and fertilizing will produce more flowers in 30–45 days.
LANDSCAPE USE Shade tolerant; excellent in shrubs such as hydrangeas, abelias, anything, really; excellent in containers. If you're into that matching-shoes-and-bag thing, grow 'King Edward VII' with *Ribes sanguineum* 'King Edward VII'. They won't ever bloom at the same time (unfortunate, given the color of the currant), but the clematis will do a splendid job of enlivening the out-of-bloom shrub.
ZONES 4–10

Clematis Kingfisher 'Evipo037'

lavender-blue, single

This clematis was bred to flower on short growth and do well in containers. It is all that. The color is rich lavender tending toward, but not quite reaching, blue. It is enhanced by leaning into dwarf blue-green conifers and gives a great display in the autumn, certainly as good as the volume of blossoms produced in the spring.

HEIGHT 6–7 feet (1.8–2 m)
LIGHT EXPOSURE Full sun, or excellent in dappled or partial shade.
PRUNING Prune by one-half in late winter for early spring bloom. Deadhead after first flowering for best rebloom, although the breeder suggests taking the whole plant back by half its height. Hard prune in winter in climates below zone 6.
BLOOM TIME First wave of blooms in late April through late May. Deadheading and fertilizing will produce more flowers in 30–45 days.
LANDSCAPE USE Shade tolerant; excellent in small shrubs; excellent in containers. This is a showstopper paired with Japanese maples that color well in the autumn, or with golden new growth in the spring. Also good with *Thujopsis dolabrata* 'Nana', and low-growing cotoneasters.
ZONES 5–10

Clematis 'King George V'

pink, single

This is a decidedly feminine pink flower to name after a man who was, as we are given to understand, a rather muscular king of England. Evidently he bullied his younger son to the point he stuttered (King George VI, who never has had a clematis named after him). The blossoms of this clematis are a fine rich pink, often lightly outlined with pale pink, and the sepal edges are wavy. The reverse surface has a strong green bar, sometimes influencing the facing view to be a darker pink, but one cannot call this flower anything like consistently barred.

HEIGHT 7–10 feet (2–3 m)

LIGHT EXPOSURE Full sun or partial shade.

PRUNING Prune by one-half in late winter for early spring bloom. Deadhead after first flowering for best rebloom. Hard prune in winter in climates below zone 6.

BLOOM TIME First wave of blooms in late April through late May. Deadheading and fertilizing will produce more flowers in 30–45 days. Excellent autumn rebloom.

LANDSCAPE USE Shade tolerant; excellent in small to medium-sized shrubs, and especially pleasing in the spring with the creamy-flowered viburnums; reasonably long-lived in containers.

ZONES 5–10

Clematis 'Kiri Te Kanawa'

purple/blue, double

This is simply the best double purple/blue clematis, and maybe the best double, period. Other than its ranginess, there is little here to be improved. The intensity of color comes from 'Beauty of Worcester', but unlike that clematis, "Kiri" is fully double every time she blooms, which she gets from her other parent, 'Chalcedony'. Unlike some double clematis that are so strident or oddly formed they really must be grown on their own, 'Kiri Te Kanawa' wanders hither and yon, binding shrubs together before the show begins. The color is exquisite whether deeply royal purple upon opening, or progressing to soft mid-blue at maturity.

HEIGHT 7–10 feet (2–3 m)
LIGHT EXPOSURE Needs full sun to produce the fullest flowers and to rebloom well.
PRUNING Prune by one-half in late winter for early spring bloom. Deadhead after first flowering for best rebloom. Hard prune in winter in climates below zone 7.
BLOOM TIME First wave of blooms in mid-May through late June. Deadheading and fertilizing will produce more flowers in about 60 days.
LANDSCAPE USE This is a rangy vine, best grown on an ample trellis or hosted by a large shrub. Forms of mock-orange (*Philadelphus*), witch hazel (*Hamamelis*), and Japanese maple (*Acer palmatum*) work well. The color of this clematis is perfect amidst autumn foliage. Think of this blue with the golden foliage and hunky hips of *Rosa rugosa*.
ZONES 4–10

Clematis 'Lady Betty Balfour'

purple, single

This offspring of 'Jackmanii' progeny 'Gipsy Queen' has two interesting features that make it well worth growing. First, it changes color. "Lady Betty" opens purple, even shading to red, and after two days or so, turns a uniform deep blue—hard to believe unless you've seen it, but it does. Second, this vine likes it hot. If you put this clematis with her feet in the shade, especially afternoon shade, she will hardly ever bloom. This clematis flowers well only with ample water and sun from the ground up.

HEIGHT 10–13 feet (3–4 m)
LIGHT EXPOSURE Full sun a must.
PRUNING Hard prune in late winter.
BLOOM TIME Truly a summer bloomer, July onward.
LANDSCAPE USE Great in big hardy fuchsias, large shrub roses, and other shrubs you might want to prune at the same time. Excellent on fences and porches.
ZONES 4–10

Clematis 'Lady Northcliffe'

lavender-blue, single

For a good, all-purpose lavender-blue large-flowered hybrid, it is hard to beat this heirloom cultivar. The color holds well in full sun, and the plant is a bit larger at maturity than 'Fujimusume', giving one more options for partnering this clematis in the garden. Like 'General Sikorski', this can open a rather strong lilac color, but it quickly becomes bluer. In my garden the vine is mainly supported by three cobalt blue balls with different textural effects on the glass, each held aloft on rebar. If they were any less blue, the flowers of this clematis would clash with the ornaments.

HEIGHT 5–10 feet (1.5–3 m)
LIGHT EXPOSURE Full sun; excellent in dappled or partial shade.
PRUNING Prune by one-half in late winter for early spring bloom. Deadhead after first flowering for best rebloom. Hard prune in winter in climates below zone 6. If grown amongst roses, prune as much or as little as the roses are pruned, at the same time of year.
BLOOM TIME First wave of blooms in late April through late May. Deadheading and fertilizing will produce more flowers in 60 days.
LANDSCAPE USE Shade tolerant; excellent in small to medium-sized shrubs and roses; too lanky for containers.
ZONES 4–10

Clematis 'Lord Nevill'

purple, single

If this antique cultivar is not one of the parents of 'Kacper', I would be very much surprised. The color here is a strikingly violent violet, with heavily textured sepal surfaces and tightly crimped edges. Some would call this a violet-blue. A short-lived red brushstroke at the base of the sepals is not unusual. In partial shade, the color might almost be called plum in the newly opened flowers, but the violet will win out.

HEIGHT 8–10 feet (2.5–3 m)
LIGHT EXPOSURE Any exposure, but the color will vary in varying light.
PRUNING Prune by one-half in late winter for early spring bloom. Deadhead after first flowering for best rebloom. Hard prune in winter in climates below zone 7.
BLOOM TIME First wave of blooms in late April through late May. Deadheading and fertilizing will produce more flowers in 30–45 days.
LANDSCAPE USE Shade tolerant; excellent in medium-sized shrubs and roses.
ZONES 5–10

Clematis 'Louise Rowe'

blue, double

One could debate whether the color of these blossoms is pale blue or pale lavender. I come down on the pale blue side. The sepals are ample and well overlapped, giving the double and semidouble flowers tremendous presence, amplified by the volume of flowers a well-grown specimen can produce. The first wave of blooms in the spring will be fully double, followed by single, semidouble, and fully double all at once in late summer or autumn.

HEIGHT 6.5–10 feet (2–3 m)
LIGHT EXPOSURE Partial shade enhances the subtle color and is well tolerated.

PRUNING Prune by one-half in late winter for early spring bloom. Deadhead after first flowering for best rebloom. Hard prune in winter in climates below zone 6.
BLOOM TIME First wave of blooms in early to late May. Deadheading and fertilizing will produce more flowers in 60 days.
LANDSCAPE USE Shade tolerant; this can be a rangy vine, best grown on an ample trellis or hosted by a forgiving, blue-foliaged conifer, to strengthen the clematis color.
ZONES 5–10

Clematis 'Madame Baron-Veillard'

pink, single

You may call her "Mad Baron" when amongst the clematis cognoscenti. This vine defies the most famous of the old wives' tales concerning clematis ("Feet in the shade, head in the sun"): it simply must have sun from the ground up in a warm aspect to flower reliably. No manner of pruning manipulation will convince it to flower before an ample dose of sunshine has ripened the wood. Plus, "Madame Baron" is a big girl. She is best draping out of a small tree or placed on a gazebo or arbor. The flower color is not entirely pink. There is a lavender cast here.

HEIGHT 13–16.5 feet (4–5 m)
LIGHT EXPOSURE Full sun is an absolute must. In coastal areas and climates with summer overcast, this will be a poor performer.
PRUNING Hard prune in late winter. Hard prune in winter in climates below zone 6.
BLOOM TIME First wave of blooms in late June through August.
LANDSCAPE USE This is a big lanky clematis that needs to gain some height before it will even think of flowering. Needs an ample structure or small tree that won't mind carrying a clematis for a few months every summer. Excellent as summer/autumn decoration for out-of-bloom lilacs.
ZONES 5–10

Clematis 'Marcelina'

purple, single

Polish clematis breeders have a way with bold colors. This cultivar proved the point in 2014, at a trial of new clematis varieties conducted at the University of Georgia for the International Clematis Society. This vine was in lush, dramatic bloom and won full marks for color and abundance. In full sun the color might best be called deep violet. The self color is violet and the bar is purple, but in a warm climate, the purple suffuses the entire sepal. One cannot think of this as a barred flower.

HEIGHT 10–13.5 feet (3–4 m)
LIGHT EXPOSURE Best in full sun.
PRUNING Considered a late large-flowered hybrid, so hard prune in winter.
BLOOM TIME First wave of blooms in June. Prune by half and fertilize to produce more flowers in 60 days.
LANDSCAPE USE Fabulous over an arch, where it can announce its presence with authority.
ZONES 4–9

Clematis 'Margaret Hunt'

pink, single

This is a favorite clematis to use as a groundcover. The starry pink flowers, tending to lilac shades in cool weather, are produced on a rangy plant capable of wandering over swaths of hardy geraniums, astrantias, and similar billowy mounding herbaceous perennials. The parentage of this vine is unknown, but given its color and habit, if 'Madame Baron-Veillard' wasn't involved, I'd be very much surprised.

HEIGHT 8–10 feet (2.5–3 m)
LIGHT EXPOSURE Must have full sun, preferably from the ground up.
PRUNING Hard prune in late winter. Deadhead by one-half the vine length after first flowering for best rebloom.
BLOOM TIME First wave of blooms in late June. Another wave will come in the autumn with some grooming and fertilizer after the first wave.
LANDSCAPE USE Unless allowed to drape out of a small tree, the upfacing flowers of this cultivar are best seen romping over mounding herbaceous perennials in full sun. Imagine *Geranium* Rozanne 'Gerwat' with this charming clematis scampering over it.
ZONES 5–10

Clematis 'Maureen'

plum, single

The color of 'Maureen' is indescribably delicious. It can be nearly claret when first open, heavily blended with plum, sometimes with the hint of a plush red bar, other times the self color is uniform and velvety throughout. One sees this listed as being purple, violet, or red. It is none of those. The flowers are rounded and plump, and then the sepal edges slump as the blossom ages. This cultivar isn't often offered in the trade, as success with cuttings is usually less than 50%. If you find it, buy it.

HEIGHT 6.5–9 feet (2–3 m)
LIGHT EXPOSURE Full sun or dappled to partial shade.
PRUNING Prune by one-half in late winter for early spring bloom. Deadhead after first flowering for best rebloom. Hard prune in winter in climates below zone 6.
BLOOM TIME First wave of blooms in late April through late May. Deadheading and fertilizing will produce more flowers in 30–45 days.
LANDSCAPE USE Shade tolerant; excellent in small shrubs; excellent in containers. My favorite combination with this clematis involves old garden roses such as 'Hebe's Lip' or 'Leda', both white with lipstick red tips or edges to the petals.
ZONES 4–10

Clematis 'Mrs. George Jackman'

white, single/semidouble

Do we list this with the doubles, or not? Although it is not uncommon, especially in the spring, for "Mrs. George," as she is familiarly known, to throw out more than eight sepals, the vine rarely produces fully double flowers on the order of a 'Vyvyan Pennell' or a 'Louise Rowe'. Later summer blooms may have the odd extra sepal, and blooms in the autumn may give you 12–15 fully formed sepals; again, cool weather during bud formation sets the stage for the number of sepals. This sturdy cultivar, another classic (1873) from the house of Jackman, is long-lived once established, with an unusual capacity to flower well into the earliest days of winter, barring an extended deep freeze.

HEIGHT 7–9 feet (2–3 m)

LIGHT EXPOSURE Excellent in dappled or partial shade, tolerates full sun, fairly hail-proof.

PRUNING Prune by one-half in late winter for early spring bloom. Deadhead after first flowering for best rebloom. Hard prune in winter in climates below zone 7.

BLOOM TIME First wave of blooms in late April through late May. Deadheading and fertilizing will produce more flowers in 30–45 days. Long autumn bloom period.

LANDSCAPE USE Shade tolerant; excellent in small to medium-sized shrubs; especially effective in broadleaf evergreens and yews.

ZONES 4–8

Clematis 'Mrs. N. Thompson'

purple with red bar, single

If you prefer your clematis rich and vividly colored, this barred clematis will suit you very well. "Mrs. N," as she is known when at home, is a luscious dark lilac enlivened by a deep red bar. In climates with slowly approaching spring weather and continuing cool nights, the color combination will remind you of a stained-glass window. The parentage is unknown, but this may be one of the few barred clematis without 'Nelly Moser' as a direct parent. Nelly's near progeny are rarely so brilliant.

HEIGHT 6.5–10 feet (2–3 m)

LIGHT EXPOSURE Tolerates shade, but better in full sun, as the color does not fade. In hot weather the color may be variable.

PRUNING Prune by one-half in late winter for early spring bloom. Deadhead after first flowering for best rebloom. Hard prune in winter in climates below zone 7.

BLOOM TIME First wave of blooms in late April through late May. Deadheading and fertilizing will produce more flowers in 30–45 days.

LANDSCAPE USE Not long-lived in containers, better used in the ground. Exceptionally handsome in gray-foliaged shrubs, such as *Pyrus salicifolia* 'Pendula' (silver weeping pear). Also seen as a pretty partner in *Rosa glauca*.

ZONES 5–10

Clematis 'Mrs. Spencer-Castle'

pink, double

No less a clematis expert than Brewster Rogerson considers this the double clematis capable of making the prettiest blossoms. We have already established my preference for double clematis resembling lush open roses. This cultivar is able to produce just such flowers: nearly perfect rosettes of soft to cotton-candy pink. There is little difference between this and 'Violet Elizabeth', with the notable exception being that 'Mrs. Spencer Castle' adds to her allure by having distinct purple veining on the undersides of the sepals. Late-season flowers may be single but are more likely to be semidouble with sufficient fertilizer and sun.

HEIGHT 6.5–13 feet (2–4 m)

LIGHT EXPOSURE Full sun to partial shade, but the most fully double flowers are produced in full sun, and it needs more light to rebloom well.

PRUNING Prune by one-half in late winter for early spring bloom. Deadhead after first flowering for best rebloom. Hard prune in winter in climates below zone 7.

BLOOM TIME First wave of blooms in mid-May through late June. Deadheading and fertilizing will produce more flowers in 60 days.

LANDSCAPE USE This can be a rangy vine, best grown on an ample trellis or hosted by larger sun-loving shrubs and roses.

ZONES 5–10

Clematis 'Negritianka'

purple, single

'Negritianka' (aka 'Negritjanka'), another great clematis to emerge from behind the Iron Curtain, hit the Western trade in the early 1990s. The name means "African girl," and the sultry dark color is just what one would expect. Although sometimes tending to violet when photographed, in person the color is a rich matte purple, quite deliciously deep. This is a vine best displayed out in the open on tall structures where the color can carry.

HEIGHT 8–10 feet (2.5–3 m)

LIGHT EXPOSURE Best in full sun.

PRUNING Hard prune in winter.

BLOOM TIME Starts as early as late May in warm spring climates. Deadheading (or taking the whole plant down by half) and fertilizing will produce more flowers in 60 days.

LANDSCAPE USE Best on tall arbors and structures where the color shows well. Too dark for partial shade, although it would grow well enough . . . it's just that the blossoms would disappear.

ZONES 5–10

Clematis 'Nelly Moser'

pink with red bar, single

This clematis is the grande dame of barred clematis. She was introduced in 1897 and has stayed in the trade undiminished ever since. Whether this brand of striping appeals to you or not, one has to give the devil her due: she is tough, long-lived, and a stellar performer in partial shade, where the color stays vivid. "Nelly" is widely used as a parent, bringing us such offspring as 'Fireworks' and 'Lincoln Star'. She passes along not only her stripes but also her tenacious longevity.

HEIGHT 6.5–13 feet (2–4 m)

LIGHT EXPOSURE Best in dappled or partial shade, well out of west or hot sun, which fades the color. Placement is everything with this cultivar.

PRUNING Prune by one-half in late winter for early spring bloom. Deadhead after first flowering for best rebloom. Hard prune in winter in climates below zone 7.

BLOOM TIME First wave of blooms in late April through late May. Deadheading and fertilizing will produce more flowers in 30–45 days. In long-season climates, three flushes of bloom are not uncommon.

LANDSCAPE USE Shade tolerant; perfect for enlivening rhododendrons, or decorating the lower legs of lilacs, where the shrub affords the clematis some shade. Too rangy for container use without constant pinching of the growing tips.

ZONES 5–10

Clematis 'Niobe'

red, single

Deep, dark, lustrous red, that's 'Niobe'. Bred in Poland during the Cold War, this clematis was spirited to England and introduced through Fisk's Nursery in 1975. It was an instant sensation. Early-season flowers are plump and intensely dark. Summer flowers in full sun are more starry in shape, and brighter red. I have read that if this is hard pruned in winter the biggest darkest flowers will be lost. This has not been my experience. As the furnishing vine for the lower trunks of my *Syringa vulgaris* 'Miss Ellen Willmott', this vine puts up about 5 feet (1.5 m) of new growth each spring and gets down to the business of flowering, no matter when or how much I prune it. The first blooms come in early May.

HEIGHT 8–10.5 feet (2.5–3 m)
LIGHT EXPOSURE Excellent in both dappled shade or full sun.
PRUNING Prune by one-half in late winter for early spring bloom. Deadhead after first flowering for best rebloom. Hard prune in winter in climates below zone 6.
BLOOM TIME First wave of blooms in late April through late May. Deadheading and fertilizing will produce more flowers in 30–45 days.
LANDSCAPE USE Shade tolerant; excellent in small to medium-sized shrubs; prune and fertilize to partner 'Niobe' with hardy hibiscus for an August full of fireworks.
ZONES 4–9

Clematis 'Omoshiro'

white with red outline, single

This is another big, decadent flower of the white-with-burgundy-pencil-edge school. It predates 'Fond Memories' and seems to come from sturdier stock. Clematis breeder Szczepan Marczynski did a side-by-side trial of 'Omoshiro' with 'Utopia', a similar Japanese cultivar, and 'Omoshiro' was by far the more vigorous and floriferous of the two. But then, 'Utopia' is half *Clematis florida*, and 'Omoshiro' is not. These flowers are bolder, with a more white background.

HEIGHT 5–10 feet (1.5–3 m)
LIGHT EXPOSURE Any exposure from full sun to partial shade.
PRUNING Prune by one-half in late winter for early spring bloom. Deadhead after first flowering for best rebloom. Hard prune in winter in climates below zone 6.
BLOOM TIME First wave of blooms in early May through early June. Deadheading and fertilizing will produce more flowers in around 45 days.
LANDSCAPE USE Shade tolerant; excellent decorating the lower branches of deciduous magnolias (*Magnolia stellata*, *M.* ×*soulangeana*), which the clematis slightly resembles.
ZONES 5–10

Clematis 'Perle d'Azur'

blue, single

Never mind that it generally flings itself about with mad abandon, this rangy, lanky cultivar has been popular since its 1885 introduction. The color of 'Perle d'Azur' resists being captured accurately in static images, even in this digital age. With slide film there was no hope. Periwinkle blue comes close to a description, and the surface is pebbled. The smallish blossoms cover the plant in midsummer, seemingly without regard to when it is pruned. The leaves are large, but the internodal distance (the amount of stem between each leaf node) is quite long, making this vine appear rather unruly. But for all that, it is a beauty.

HEIGHT 10–13.5 feet (3–4 m)
LIGHT EXPOSURE Best in full sun to produce the most blooms.
PRUNING Hard prune in late winter for midsummer bloom. Deadhead after first flowering for best rebloom. Hard prune in winter in climates below zone 6.
BLOOM TIME First wave of blooms in early June to mid-July. Deadheading and fertilizing will produce more flowers in approximately 45 days.
LANDSCAPE USE Effective with climbing roses, in small trees, and then there's that stunning half-round wall at Sissinghurst Castle, which hosts seven crowns of 'Perle d'Azur'. Together, they are perhaps the most photographed clematis in the world.
ZONES 5–10

Clematis 'Perrin's Pride'

purple, single

This plump flower is always described as dusky purple, and so it should be. The sepal surfaces are slightly pebbled, and the color is a strong purple, matte and subdued slightly by an interestingly dusky quality. That, and the broad rounded sepals make this cultivar quite easy to pick out of a crowd. Not many large-flowered hybrid clematis have come from the United States, and this is certainly one of the very best of those august few. This plant has been wrongly attributed to the Viticella Group. Its looks, bloom time, and parentage listed in *An Illustrated Encyclopedia of Clematis* (Toomey and Leeds 2001) say otherwise.

HEIGHT 8–10 feet (2.5–3 m)
LIGHT EXPOSURE Full sun or partial shade.
PRUNING Prune by one-half in late winter for early spring bloom. Deadhead after first flowering for best rebloom. Hard prune in winter in climates below zone 7.
BLOOM TIME First wave of blooms in late April through late May. Deadheading and fertilizing will produce more flowers in 30–45 days.
LANDSCAPE USE Shade tolerant; excellent for decorating the lower stems of woody climbers such as wisteria and roses, as long as root competition is avoided.
ZONES 5–10

Clematis 'Peveril Pearl'

lavender, single

If you have a place for a subtle, soft lavender clematis with little pretension to blue, here's your best choice. The blossoms can be 9 inches (23 cm) in diameter, and the color blends marvelously with other clematis. I am particularly fond of using these big flowers juxtaposed with *Clematis crispa*, which is generally the same color in a small, curly bell. 'Peveril Pearl' has excellent rebloom and attractive seedheads.

HEIGHT 6–8 feet (1.8–2.5 m)
LIGHT EXPOSURE Best in dappled or partial shade.
PRUNING Prune by one-half in late winter for early spring bloom. Deadhead after first flowering for best rebloom. Hard prune in winter in climates below zone 7.
BLOOM TIME First wave of blooms in late April through late May. Deadheading and fertilizing will produce more flowers in 30–45 days.
LANDSCAPE USE Shade tolerant; excellent in the lower stems of shrub roses; too rangy for containers. Ethereal dancing as a groundcover over blue-green hostas, or flowering with hostas with lavender flowers.
ZONES 5–10

Clematis 'Piilu' Little Duckling ❇

pink with red bar, single

As legend has it, this cultivar was so beloved of its breeder, Uno Kivistik, he requested it be planted on his grave. The trade name is the translation of the Estonian cultivar name—there! You have learned a word of Estonian. The flowers are of small diameter for a large-flowered hybrid, and can be double when grown in cold climates or at high elevations with short seasons. Where this author gardens, we rarely see so much as an extra sepal, but the prolific flower production makes up for this lack. 'Piilu' is amply capable of obscuring its foliage with the profusion of its blooms.

HEIGHT 3.5–6.5 feet (1–2 m)
LIGHT EXPOSURE Prefers lots of sun with sufficient water.

PRUNING Prune by one-half in late winter for early spring bloom. Deadhead after first flowering for best rebloom. Hard prune in winter in climates below zone 6.
BLOOM TIME First wave of blooms in late April through late May. Deadheading and fertilizing will produce more flowers in 45–60 days.
LANDSCAPE USE One of the best clematis for containers ever, it stays dense and short. It tolerates shallow-rooted annuals around its feet. One of the most effective uses I've seen was 'Piilu' in the center of a half whiskey barrel with a froth of marguerite daisies around the edge of the container—very casual and exuberant.
ZONES 5–10

Clematis Rebecca 'Evipo016'

red, single

Many consider Rebecca one of the best red clematis ever produced, and certainly the best from Raymond Evison. I prefer Rosemoor 'Evipo002', but only because I have more history with it, and it establishes more quickly. This hybrid comes close to being truly red, and the velvet sheen lasts almost as long as the flower itself. The stamens are unique in having red connectives, the structure holding the two halves of the anther together. This kind of detail is the mark of the nuanced eye of a practiced plant breeder.

HEIGHT 6–7 feet (1.8–2 m)
LIGHT EXPOSURE Full sun or partial shade. Color is better in full sun.
PRUNING Prune by one-half in late winter for early spring bloom. Deadhead after first flowering for best rebloom. Hard prune in winter in climates below zone 6.
BLOOM TIME First wave of blooms in late April through late May. Deadheading and fertilizing will produce more flowers in 30–45 days.
LANDSCAPE USE Excellent in small shrubs; excellent in containers. Can be used to good effect growing in a container in front of a taller, purple clematis in the ground, perhaps 'Viola' or similar, since both would have a satiny finish on the sepals, for a saturated jewel-tone combination.
ZONES 5–10

Clematis 'Pinky'

pink with red bar, single

One of the prettiest barred clematis to come out of Japan, 'Pinky' has bloomed better in a challenging garden position (competing with the Montana Group's 'Margaret Jones' on a split-rail fence) than in more open ground adorning *Hypericum ×inodorum* 'Summergold'. Best grown in partial shade to preserve the soft background pink from the sun. Interestingly, 'Pinky' is starting to make the rounds in the cut flower trade.

HEIGHT 4–7 feet (1.2–2 m)
LIGHT EXPOSURE Excellent in dappled or partial shade.
PRUNING Prune by one-half in late winter for early spring bloom. Deadhead after first flowering for best rebloom. Hard prune in winter in climates below zone 7.
BLOOM TIME First wave of blooms in late April through late May. Deadheading and fertilizing will produce more flowers in 30–45 days.
LANDSCAPE USE Shade tolerant; excellent in small shrubs. Lower stems might get too bare to be pleasing in containers.
ZONES 5–10

Clematis Reflections 'Evipo035'
lavender, double center

The subtlety of this color—imagine a lavender-mauve dawn reflected in water—is enhanced by an unusual form of doubling, which is limited to just a few clematis cultivars. The double staminodes are perfectly placed between the outermost sepals, and are shorter. They are also slightly ruffled and variable in length relative to each other, making for a more open center with dark anthers. The whole is a lovely, rather insouciant and utterly charming flower.

HEIGHT 4–6 feet (1.2–1.8 m)
LIGHT EXPOSURE Partial shade to full sun. Partial shade preserves the color.
PRUNING Prune by one-half in late winter for early spring bloom. Deadhead after first flowering for best rebloom. Hard prune in winter in climates below zone 7.
BLOOM TIME First wave of blooms in mid-May to mid-June. Deadheading and fertilizing will produce more flowers in 30–45 days.
LANDSCAPE USE More compact than most double clematis, so better suited to containers or low-growing broadleaf evergreens like many daphnes.
ZONES 5–10

Clematis 'Rhapsody'
blue, single

Although there was an initial confusion (two clematis were given the name at the same time), this name is rightly applied to Barry Fretwell's stellar blue large-flowered hybrid, which is widely available in the trade and justifiably popular. The sepals are slender and pointed. The surface is pebbled. New flowers might seem purple but quickly settle into a nearly neon, brilliant mid-blue. Even digital images do not do it justice. The color can be slightly paler along the midrib.

HEIGHT 6–13 feet (1.8–4 m)
LIGHT EXPOSURE Color is best in full sun.
PRUNING Prune by one-half in late winter for early spring bloom. Deadhead after first flowering for best rebloom. Hard prune in winter in climates below zone 6.
BLOOM TIME First wave of blooms in mid-May through late June. Deadheading and fertilizing will produce more flowers in 30–45 days.
LANDSCAPE USE Excellent in shrubs and roses; capable of being a real diva on a solo trellis.
ZONES 5–10

Clematis 'Roko-Kolla'

white, single

Estonian clematis breeder Uno Kivistik is responsible for many white large-flowered hybrids, but this is the one to which I give full marks. The reverse of the flower has a strong persistent green bar—typical of hybrids derived from *Clematis patens*—and it gives the upper surface a fresh "not quite ripe" color, even in hot weather. The incised midribs are distinct in this flower, breaking up the creamy white with a touch of texture and directing the eye to the similarly-colored stamens. The flowers are not huge, but they are intensely interesting and deserving of a placement in the garden where they might be closely inspected. The sepals are pointed, giving a lighter, starry effect.

HEIGHT 5–7 feet (1.5–2 m)
LIGHT EXPOSURE Excellent in full sun or partial shade.
PRUNING Prune by one-half in late winter for early spring bloom. Deadhead after first flowering for best rebloom. Hard prune in winter in climates below zone 7.
BLOOM TIME First wave of blooms in late May through June. Deadheading and fertilizing will produce more flowers in 30–45 days.
LANDSCAPE USE Shade tolerant; excellent in small shrubs and roses; excellent in containers. Tends to flower on the last 2–3 feet (0.5–1 m) of the stems.
ZONES 5–10

Clematis Rosemoor 'Evipo002'

red, single

This cultivar predates some of the much-touted new reds from Raymond Evison but is still my favorite red from him. The color does not fade, the depth of color is sumptuous, and the plant has several garden uses. If you fancy a red exclamation point, grow Rosemoor alone on a tuteur. It is a shade of red that pairs well with autumn colors, particularly those of certain *Acer palmatum* selections, without overwhelming its host.

HEIGHT 6.5–8 feet (2–2.5 m)
LIGHT EXPOSURE Good in full sun or dappled shade.
PRUNING Prune by one-half in late winter for early spring bloom. Deadhead after first flowering for best rebloom. Hard prune in winter in climates below zone 7.
BLOOM TIME First wave of blooms in late April through late May. Deadheading and fertilizing will produce more flowers in 30–45 days.
LANDSCAPE USE Excellent in small to medium-sized shrubs and shrub roses; excellent in containers. Can get bare-legged if left unpruned.
ZONES 4–9

Clematis 'Rouge Cardinal'

red, single

This hybrid from the 1960s is still widely available in commerce and for good reason. The color is yummy, and it can be grown for spring or summer bloom, giving it a great variety of garden uses. On tours to visit gardens, I'm always pleasantly surprised to ask what a particularly gorgeous red clematis is, and to be told, "Oh, that's just 'Rouge Cardinal'." *Just* . . . Faint praise for a plant that never fails to impress. Perhaps my favorite use of this plant is in the garden of Portland, Oregon, garden writer Dulcy Mahar. She paired it with *Hydrangea macrophylla* 'Glowing Embers', for a truly showstopping pop of color in late summer.

HEIGHT 6.5–13 feet (2–4 m)
LIGHT EXPOSURE Full sun or partial shade.
PRUNING Hard prune or prune by one-half in late winter for early spring bloom. Deadhead after first flowering for best rebloom. Hard prune in winter in climates below zone 6.
BLOOM TIME First wave of blooms in late May if half pruned in late winter. Deadheading and fertilizing will produce more flowers in 45 days.
LANDSCAPE USE Too rangy for containers, but otherwise amenable to whatever is asked of it.
ZONES 5–10

Clematis 'Rüütel'

red, single

This hybrid is a more fully saturated deep pink than its parent 'Ernest Markham'. The plant size is more compact, so if you want this color in the garden but not the lankiness of 'Ernest Markham', you couldn't do better. The sepals are somewhat narrow but have an attractively waved edge. Pronunciation is **roo**-tl, not roo-**tel**.

HEIGHT 3.5–10 feet (1–3 m)

LIGHT EXPOSURE Full sun to dappled shade.

PRUNING Prune by one-half in late winter for early spring bloom. Deadhead after first flowering for best rebloom. Hard prune in winter in climates below zone 6.

BLOOM TIME First wave of blooms in late April through late May. Deadheading and fertilizing will produce more flowers in 30–45 days.

LANDSCAPE USE Shade tolerant; excellent in small shrubs. Tolerates life in a container graciously, and rarely complains. My 'Rüütel' is in a container; I move the pot around the garden, placing the clematis where I need emphasis.

ZONES 5–10

Clematis 'Semu'

purple, single

The first time I laid eyes on this clematis was in the garden of Roy Nunn in Cambridge, England. I was with Maurice Horn, of Oregon's Joy Creek Nursery. We stared. We swooned. We had to have it. 'Semu' blossoms can only be called curvaceous. The color is distinctly violet as the flowers open, gradually fading to blue, giving the whole plant, which blooms brilliantly from the ground up, a multi-shaded effect that is literally jaw-dropping. I know it dropped mine and Maurice's, too. Roy had it in a large container with a tuteur. The flowers were top-to-bottom, all the way around. A knockout!

HEIGHT 7–10.5 feet (2–3 m)
LIGHT EXPOSURE Full sun or partial shade.
PRUNING Prune by one-half in late winter for early spring bloom. Deadhead after first flowering for best rebloom. Hard prune in winter in climates below zone 7.
BLOOM TIME First wave of blooms in late April through late May. Deadheading and fertilizing will produce more flowers in 30–45 days.
LANDSCAPE USE Shade tolerant; excellent in small shrubs; outstanding in large containers. Pairs exceedingly well with yellow, peach, and orange roses.
ZONES 5–10

Clematis 'Snow Queen'

white, single

If you want an excellent dark-eyed white clematis for containers, you cannot do better than 'Snow Queen'. Something in the texture and contrast of this flower, which may appear a touch lavender when it first opens, is irresistible. It flowers from the ground up, especially if new growth is pinched when the plant is 2–3 feet (0.5–1 m) tall. On a sale bench with other white clematis in bloom, this one will sell out first. I put it down to the heavily mascaraed eye of dark anthers. There is a pleasingly crimped quality to the edges of the pointed sepals.

HEIGHT 8–10 feet (2.5–3 m)
LIGHT EXPOSURE Excellent in dappled or partial shade.
PRUNING Prune by one-half in late winter for early spring bloom. Deadhead after first flowering for best rebloom. Hard prune in winter in climates below zone 7.
BLOOM TIME First wave of blooms in late April through late May. Deadheading and fertilizing will produce more flowers in 30–45 days.
LANDSCAPE USE Shade tolerant; excellent in small shrubs; excellent in containers if pinched for bushiness.
ZONES 5–10

Clematis 'Solidarnosc'

red, single

This is my favorite Polish red clematis, rising above some very stiff competition ('Monte Cassino', 'Westerplatte', and the famous 'Niobe', to name three). I've said elsewhere the Polish breeders have a flair for the dramatic, and Szczepan Marczynski proves the rule. In addition to being fabulously, brilliantly, daringly red (especially in hot weather), this cultivar flowers well in containers and makes a perfect column of itself, blooming from the ground up. It is named for the Polish trade union (of which Szczepan was a member) that defied the communist regime, leading to the ultimate liberation of much of Eastern Europe.

HEIGHT 3.5–5 feet (1–1.5 m)
LIGHT EXPOSURE Full sun or partial shade.
PRUNING Prune by one-half in late winter for early spring bloom. Deadhead after first flowering for best rebloom. Hard prune in winter in climates below zone 7.
BLOOM TIME First wave of blooms in late April through late May. Deadheading and fertilizing will produce more flowers in 30–45 days.
LANDSCAPE USE Shade tolerant; excellent in small shrubs; excellent in containers. Mine is in a large pot with *Hosta* 'Osprey' at its feet. Although 'Solidarnosc' has a handsome tripod to climb on, it typically wanders over to the dwarf repeat-flowering lilac (*Syringa* Tinkerbelle 'Bailbelle') in the adjacent pot.
ZONES 4–10

Clematis 'Tenri no Asagasumi'

white with lavender outline, single

This generously flowering cultivar represents another color combination that defies categorization. The flower is generally quite pale, nearly white, with a broad blue-lavender edge. In cold weather this border is quite distinct and the color concentrated. In warm weather it is more of a lavender blush. As with so many Japanese names, the translation is charming and evocative: "morning mist at Tenri." The lighter to white central color gives the flower a full look, kind of an optical illusion.

HEIGHT to 8 feet (2.5 m)

LIGHT EXPOSURE Excellent in dappled or partial shade. Full sun fades the color.

PRUNING Prune by one-half in late winter for early spring bloom. Deadhead after first flowering for best rebloom. Hard prune in winter in climates below zone 7.

BLOOM TIME First wave of blooms in late April through late May. Deadheading and fertilizing will produce more flowers in 30–45 days.

LANDSCAPE USE Shade tolerant; excellent in small shrubs and columnar structures and posts. It has excellent autumn rebloom, so think about combinations of this flower with colorful foliage.

ZONES 5–9

Clematis 'Teshio'

lavender-blue, double

This double is distinguished by the strongly acuminate (pointy) light blue sepals. Even the outermost "true" sepals are gracefully tapering. The color is a medium to light lavender-blue, which marries well with yellow or white variegated foliage. Teshio is a Japanese river and coastal town, on the northernmost tip of the island of Hokkaido, and I imagine these watery environs inspired this cultivar's name. These flowers are always at least semidouble, and often very full.

HEIGHT 5–10.5 feet (1.5–3 m)
LIGHT EXPOSURE Partial shade to full sun. Partial shade preserves the color.
PRUNING Prune by one-half in late winter for early spring bloom. Deadhead after first flowering for best rebloom. Hard prune in winter in climates below zone 7.
BLOOM TIME First wave of blooms in mid-May to mid-June. Deadheading and fertilizing will produce more flowers in 60 days.
LANDSCAPE USE Shade tolerant; growth is rather rangy, so this clematis is best used on a trellis or medium to large shrub. Lovely texture combination with *Viburnum opulus* 'Roseum', and lovely color combination with the foliage of *Cornus mas* 'Variegata'.
ZONES 5–9

Clematis 'The President' ✤

purple, single

This heirloom clematis has remained popular since its introduction in 1876. The rich purple flowers are produced in two big helpings, spring and autumn. Although it hates container culture and will not survive in even the largest pot for more than two years, its uses in the ground make it exceptionally versatile.

HEIGHT 7–13 feet (2–4 m)
LIGHT EXPOSURE Full sun to dappled shade or northern exposure.
PRUNING Prune by one-half in late winter for early spring bloom. Deadhead after first flowering for best rebloom. Hard prune in winter in climates below zone 7.
BLOOM TIME First wave of blooms in late April through late May. Deadheading and fertilizing will produce more flowers in 60 days.
LANDSCAPE USE Shade tolerant; excellent in small to medium-sized shrubs, and classic in shrub roses. Also makes a lovely, richly colored groundcover. Great on fences as a backdrop for complementary-colored plants.
ZONES 5–10

Clematis 'Toki' ▾

white, single

This hybrid offers a big plump flower. If size matters, only 'Henryi' can equal the diameter of a well-grown blossom of 'Toki'. Toki is a city on Japan's Honshu Island near which *Clematis patens* can still be found growing wild, and the influence of that species is seen here with the green reverse bar and the grooved furrows down the face of the sepals. These vertical lines add to the impression of size. 'Toki' has broad overlapping sepals that are only slightly pointed. The seed tails are quite uncommonly golden, some of the prettiest of the large-flowered group.

HEIGHT 6–7 feet (1.8–2 m)
LIGHT EXPOSURE Excellent in dappled or partial shade.
PRUNING Prune by one-half in late winter for early spring bloom. Deadhead after first flowering for best rebloom. Hard prune in winter in climates below zone 7.
BLOOM TIME First wave of blooms in late April through late May. Deadheading and fertilizing will produce more flowers in 30–45 days.
LANDSCAPE USE Shade tolerant; excellent in small shrubs; excellent in containers.
ZONES 5–10

Clematis 'Tsuzuki' ▸

white, single

How many white clematis does the world need? The number is ridiculously infinite it seems, but if I had to cull the herd, I would never reject 'Tsuzuki'. This is by far the best white for container culture. This vine flowers amply from the ground up and accepts the challenges of life in a pot better than most. When you read on a plant tag that a clematis flowers early and has a mature height of less than 8 feet (2.5 m), you know you have a winner. Flower diameter 5–6 inches (12–15 cm).

HEIGHT 6–7 feet (1.8–2 m)
LIGHT EXPOSURE Excellent in dappled or partial shade.
PRUNING Prune by one-half in late winter for early spring bloom. Deadhead after first flowering for best rebloom. Hard prune in winter in climates below zone 7.
BLOOM TIME First wave of blooms in late April through late May. Deadheading and fertilizing will produce more flowers in 30–45 days.
LANDSCAPE USE Shade tolerant; excellent in small shrubs; excellent in containers.
ZONES 5–10

Clematis Vancouver 'Morning Mist' ▾

pink, single

This plant, one of the early introductions from Canada's Clearview Horticultural Products' Vancouver series, is capable of producing the largest flowers I've ever measured on a clematis, 11 inches (28 cm) wide! The flowers are pale pink, sometimes a suitably misty lavender-pink.

HEIGHT 8–12 feet (2.5–3.5 m)

LIGHT EXPOSURE Morning sun or dappled to partial shade all day. The color is subtle and fades easily.

PRUNING Prune by one-half in late winter for early spring bloom. Deadhead after first flowering for best rebloom. Hard prune in winter in climates below zone 6.

BLOOM TIME First wave of blooms in early May through early June. Deadheading and fertilizing will produce more flowers in 30–45 days.

LANDSCAPE USE Shade tolerant; too leggy to show to good effect in a container even with tip pinching. Combine with dark-foliaged conifers or broadleaf evergreens. Maybe this might be a flashy summer bauble for an out-of-bloom camellia?

ZONES 5–10

Clematis 'Veronica's Choice'

lavender, double

In partial shade, this double will produce fewer, although bigger, pale lavender flowers, tipped or streaked with a rosier hue. In full sun, the color will bleach to white within a day or two of opening (the rosy detailing will persist), but you will have many more blossoms. As with its parent 'Vyvyan Pennell', the breadth of the outermost sepals make this one of the largest doubles in sheer diameter, and with heavy feedings, the inner petaloid stamens will be profuse and rose petal–like. There is also a ruffled edge to both sepals and petaloid stamens, giving the whole flower a wonderfully fluffy effect.

HEIGHT 6.5–10 feet (2–3 m)

LIGHT EXPOSURE Tolerates partial shade well, which enhances the subtle color.

PRUNING Prune by one-half in late winter for early spring bloom. Deadhead after first flowering for best rebloom. Hard prune in winter in climates below zone 6.

BLOOM TIME First wave of blooms in early to late May, lasting into June. Deadheading and fertilizing will produce more flowers in 60 days.

LANDSCAPE USE Shade tolerant; great for a columnar effect on a pole enrobed with chicken wire or fencing cloth. Early and consistent pinching of the newest growth will produce a plant with dense foliage and flowers from the ground up, given sufficient fertilizer.

ZONES 5–9

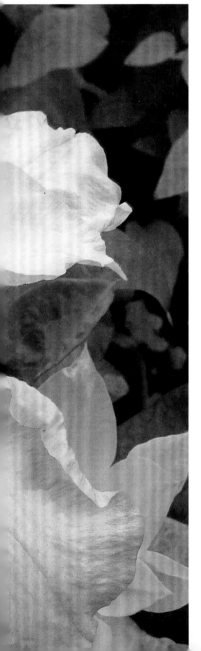

Clematis 'Victoria'

purple, single

This cultivar can best be thought of as a light violet version of 'Perle d'Azur'. Its flowers have the same shape and texture. The flower timing and need for ample light is the same, too. This is considered a late-flowering hybrid, and it is wonderful on wire fencing behind summer-blooming herbaceous perennials such as long-blooming alstroemeria, daylilies, and penstemon. This is a durable vine.

HEIGHT 10.5–13 feet (3–4 m)
LIGHT EXPOSURE Best in full sun or western exposures.
PRUNING Hard prune in late winter.
BLOOM TIME Typically has one long wave of bloom from late June/early July well into September.
LANDSCAPE USE A sterling performer on wire fencing, over arches, and in small trees. Makes a very handsome backdrop in herbaceous perennial borders.
ZONES 5–10

Clematis 'Ville de Lyon'

red, single

This was one of the first cultivars to show the direct influence of *Clematis texensis* in the creation of the red large-flowered hybrids. Because it is honestly raspberry red with a lighter bar, it retains an old-fashioned charm that marries well with cottage gardens and the flowers grown in them. Much to my surprise, this clematis even competes favorably with raspberry plants, and the berries ripening when the clematis is in flower is nothing short of mouthwatering!

HEIGHT 8–16.5 feet (2.5–5 m)
LIGHT EXPOSURE Full sun or partial shade.

PRUNING Either hard prune or reduce by one-half in late winter. Deadhead after first flowering for best rebloom. Hard prune in winter in climates below zone 6.
BLOOM TIME First wave of blooms in late April through late May if only partially pruned in winter. Deadheading and fertilizing will produce more flowers in 30–45 days. Bloom periods are long, and flower production is profuse.
LANDSCAPE USE 'Ville de Lyon' is too big for containers. Other than that, use it as you wish. Combine with climbing roses, send it up a small tree, or allow it to run along the tops of herbaceous perennials. Heavenly when it wanders into the peonies in mid-May.
ZONES 5–10

Clematis 'Voluceau'

red, single

Here's my 'Voluceau' story: in September 2008 I visited the Brooklyn Botanic Garden's Cranford Rose Garden. The area looked tired, the roses were mildewed and spent. Yet on one arbor in the middle of the garden, a beacon of deep red was glowing like a ruby—'Voluceau'. Fast forward to early June 2014. Same garden, different season. I went to that middle arbor and there was 'Voluceau'—very likely the same plant—blooming just as vigorously as when I first saw it, six years earlier. This plant is the darker red sibling of 'Rouge Cardinal', from the same breeder. Need I say more?

HEIGHT 8–10 feet (2.5–3 m)
LIGHT EXPOSURE Best in full sun. At home, mine is in the dappled shade of an apple tree, and the color is almost too dark to be effective.
PRUNING Hard prune or prune by one-half in late winter for early spring bloom. Deadhead after first flowering for best rebloom. Hard prune in winter in climates below zone 6.
BLOOM TIME First wave of blooms in late May. Deadheading and fertilizing will produce more flowers in 30–45 days.
LANDSCAPE USE Grow on arbors and tuteurs, great with roses (obviously), combines well with medium to large shrubs.
ZONES 5–10

Clematis 'Vyvyan Pennell'

mauve/blue, double

Although the parents of this plant are both purple/blue, when these double flowers open, they are what I can best describe as my idea of mauve. With sufficient fertilizer given in March and April, the buds will be fat and reveal a dense display of petaloid stamens when they open in May. After a few days, parental influence takes hold, and as the flowers age, they turn more blue. It is rather a surprising effect. More than once I've fielded queries from gardeners who don't wander outside until the color shift has occurred, and they bring their flowers in for identification. In late summer when the single flowers are produced (having no extra sepals), the flower stays rosy mauve without ever turning blue before sepal-fall.

HEIGHT 6–13 feet (1.8–4 m)
LIGHT EXPOSURE Tolerates partial shade well, without sacrificing the volume of flowers.
PRUNING Prune by one-half in late winter for early spring bloom. Deadhead after first flowering for best rebloom. Hard prune in winter in climates below zone 6.
BLOOM TIME First wave of blooms in early to late May. Deadheading and fertilizing will produce more flowers in 60 days.
LANDSCAPE USE Shade tolerant; this can be a rangy vine, best grown on an ample trellis or along a wire fence. Nice with such fellow vines as *Vitis vinifera* 'Purpurea', as long as root competition is avoided.
ZONES 5–10

Clematis 'Warszawska Nike' Midnight Showers ✤

plum, single

This is another cultivar from Brother Stefan Franczak of Poland that defies description. It is variously called "red-purple," "violet-red," "velvety red-violet," or "dark purple-violet." A Dutch clematis breeder seeing the plant in full bloom in my garden said, "It's not red enough. In Europe it is more red." What are we to make of this? The color, however you may choose to describe it, is dark and dramatic. The flower texture shifts from a satin sheen upon first opening to a more pebbled denim as the sepals age.

HEIGHT 6–7 feet (1.8–2 m)

LIGHT EXPOSURE Excellent in dappled or partial shade.

PRUNING Hard prune for summer blooms or prune by one-half in late winter for early spring bloom. Deadhead after first flowering for best rebloom. Hard prune in winter in climates below zone 6.

BLOOM TIME First wave of blooms in May through mid-June. Deadheading and fertilizing will produce more flowers in 30–45 days.

LANDSCAPE USE Shade tolerant; excellent in spring-flowering viburnums, especially those like *Viburnum opulus* 'Compactum' with a creamy lacecap hydrangea–like flower cluster. With this clematis you get a nice textural combination as well as complementary coloring.

ZONES 5–10

Clematis 'Warszawska Olga'

pink, single

Not only is this lovely flower brilliantly pink, the filaments of the stamens are, too. The anthers are bright yellow, and the whole effect is utterly bright-eyed. This is one of the final introductions to come out of the stable of Brother Stefan Franczak of Poland, and although it's making its way into the trade slowly, it has all the makings of a classic. The flowers may be darker rose pink at the margins, and the sepal edges have a cheerful crinkle.

HEIGHT 6.5–8 feet (2–2.5 m)
LIGHT EXPOSURE Excellent in dappled or partial shade, but color holds well in full sun.
PRUNING Prune by one-half in late winter for early spring bloom. Deadhead after first flowering for best rebloom. Hard prune in winter in climates below zone 6.
BLOOM TIME First wave of blooms in late April through late May. Deadheading and fertilizing will produce more flowers in 30–45 days.
LANDSCAPE USE Shade tolerant; excellent in small shrubs such as either burgundy- or yellow-foliaged berberis, where the clematis can amble over the top. This plant is quite willing to grow horizontally as a groundcover.
ZONES 5–10

Clematis 'W. E. Gladstone'

lavender-blue, single

For many years after its 1881 introduction, this long-lived and sturdy hybrid was known for having the largest flowers of any clematis. The sepals are a uniform blue (well, more blue than lavender) with a smooth surface, curvy edges, and dark eyes—a smoldering beast. This clematis deserves much more attention than it gets. Just because it has been superseded as largest, doesn't mean it isn't still wildly handsome.

HEIGHT 7–13 feet (2–4 m)
LIGHT EXPOSURE Excellent in dappled or partial shade. Does not fade much in full sun.
PRUNING Prune by one-half in late winter for early spring bloom. Deadhead after first flowering for best rebloom. Hard prune in winter in climates below zone 6.
BLOOM TIME First wave of blooms in late April through late May. Deadheading and fertilizing will produce more flowers in 45 days (the second wave is usually in July) and a big burst in early autumn.
LANDSCAPE USE Shade tolerant; excellent in mophead hydrangeas, dwarf conifers, large shrub roses. Especially nice with red-foliaged berberis. Too lanky for containers.
ZONES 4–10

Clematis 'Wildfire'

purple with red bar, single

It takes little stretch of the imagination to believe 'Mrs. N. Thompson' is the seed parent of this flashy modern cultivar from Poland. The other parent must be something dark and rich, with the persistent sheen of silk velvet, for it is this shimmering lustre that distinguishes this cultivar. Imagine "Mrs. N" with a deeper, royal purple self and a thrillingly red bar, flaunting a texture than begs tactile appreciation.

HEIGHT 7–10 feet (2–3 m)

LIGHT EXPOSURE Flowers equally well in sun or partial shade, but shows off better with more light.

PRUNING Prune by one-half in late winter for early spring bloom. Deadhead after first flowering for best rebloom. Hard prune in winter in climates below zone 6.

BLOOM TIME First wave of blooms in late April through late May. Deadheading and fertilizing will produce more flowers in 30–45 days.

LANDSCAPE USE In partial shade, give it a light background to enhance the effect of the dark colors; perhaps allow it to be a groundcover through and over gray-blue hostas. Excellent in medium-sized shrubs in full sun, particularly larger weigelas with red flowers (*Weigela* 'Bristol Ruby' springs to mind) or perhaps a variegated mock-orange, such as *Philadelphus* 'Innocence'. In either case, the clematis will flower when the shrub does, and flower again later in the season to enliven the shrubs again. Not a long-lived choice for containers.

ZONES 5–10

Clematis 'Will Barron'▾

lavender-blue, single

Will Barron was one of the founders of Clearview Horticultural Products in British Columbia, Canada. The vine named after him is one of the few "blue" clematis that may be pruned either by half in winter to start blooming in May or hard pruned to start its show a month later. The flowers are similar in color to 'Will Goodwin', but this flower has smooth edges.

HEIGHT 8–10 feet (2.5–3 m)

LIGHT EXPOSURE Excellent in dappled or partial shade.

PRUNING Prune by one-half in late winter for early spring bloom, or hard prune to start later blooming cycle. Deadhead after first flowering for best rebloom. Hard prune in winter in climates below zone 6.

BLOOM TIME First wave of blooms in late April through late May. Deadheading and fertilizing will produce more flowers in 30–45 days.

LANDSCAPE USE Shade tolerant; excellent in small trees such as Japanese snowbell (*Styrax japonicus*) or golden chain tree (*Laburnum anagyroides*). Let the clematis grow all the way to the top, and prune only every 2–3 years for the clematis to bloom with these trees, then fertilize the clematis to encourage later bloom.

ZONES 5–10

Clematis 'Will Goodwin'

lavender-blue, single

Although this plant may take a year or two to establish, and you must resist the urge to move it in the meantime (thus setting it back), it is a very satisfying flower to grow. It produces masses of wide, strongly upfacing blossoms of a clear lavender-blue with piecrust-crimped edges to the thick sepals. The effect is quite opulent. Because the flowers face the sky, if you let this vine attain its mature height you will either need a viewing platform to see its face, or you must accept the view of the green bar on the reverse of the sepals with very little blue. When buds form during a cold spring, some double flowers may be produced.

HEIGHT 8–13 feet (2.5–4 m)
LIGHT EXPOSURE Excellent in dappled or partial shade.
PRUNING Prune by one-half in late winter for early spring bloom. Deadhead after first flowering for best rebloom. Hard prune in winter in climates below zone 7.
BLOOM TIME First wave of blooms in late April through late May. Deadheading and fertilizing will produce more flowers in 45 days.
LANDSCAPE USE Shade tolerant; excellent as a groundcover if given no vertical options. Good decoration for out-of-bloom rhododendrons.
ZONES 5–10

Clematis Wisley 'Evipo001'

purple, single

This modern-day 'Jackmanii' type is a great addition to the pantheon of clematis preferring a lot of light. Perhaps a bit slow to establish, this free-flowering hybrid is a rollicking summer bloomer, well able to keep pace with the yellow bells of the Tangutica/Orientalis Group clematis, with whom it combines well. The color is violet tending to light purple. It is no surprise this clematis is Raymond Evison's "001" plant, named after the Royal Horticultural Society's flagship garden, Wisley. This is destined to become a classic. Please note the pronunciation is **whiz**-lee, not **wise**-lee.

HEIGHT 8–10.5 feet (2.5–3 m)
LIGHT EXPOSURE Best in full sun.
PRUNING Hard prune in winter, and prune by half after first wave of bloom for another autumn show.
BLOOM TIME First wave of blooms in late May to early July. Pruning and fertilizing will produce more flowers in 45 days.
LANDSCAPE USE Makes a great partner for the summer-blooming small-flowered hybrid clematis, such as 'Bill MacKenzie', 'Princess Diana', 'Betty Corning', and any of the viticellas.
ZONES 4–10

SMALL-FLOWERED HYBRIDS, SELECTIONS, AND SPECIES

Clematis 'Abundance' ❀
Viticella Group, deciduous vine

It is hard not to be fond of a plant so aptly named. The light red/cherry pink flowers are produced in tsunami-like waves. It is possible to induce two big displays in temperate climates, with long growing seasons. This is a vine of glorious vigor.

HEIGHT 9–12 feet (3–3.5 m)
LIGHT EXPOSURE Mid- to full sun; especially fine in hot afternoon sun. Shaded roots preferred, but with enough water, it will tolerate sun from the ground up.
PRUNING Hard prune to 1 foot (30 cm) in late winter.
BLOOM TIME After hard pruning in winter, flowers in July/August. This plant responds well to manipulation of standard pruning advice. If pruned by one-half its length after the first wave of bloom and fertilized, it will rebloom from autumn to frost in temperate climates. Usually 30 days to rebloom after pruning on Bastille Day (14 July).
LANDSCAPE USE This vine makes a superior column on a post that has been wrapped with fencing cloth. Also a great choice for small deciduous trees (think magnolias, semi-dwarf fruit trees) and large shrubs.
ZONES 3–11

Clematis addisonii
herbaceous perennial

This species hails from a mere two counties in the state of Virginia. Although it is limited in the wild, it takes to garden cultivation with charming alacrity. This plant will want its pH raised in regions with acidic soil and will appreciate gravel mulch in rainy climates. The leaves are rotund and somewhat fleshy. The tailored bell flowers are mahogany to deep pink, with thick sepals showing a distinct creamy interior at the margins. The outer surface is quite smooth compared to its closest cousins.

HEIGHT 5–30 inches (12–75 cm)
LIGHT EXPOSURE Partial shade, half day of direct sun. In the wild, this grows along the margins of deciduous woodlands and the verges of newly cut roads.

PRUNING Reduce to 2 inches (5 cm) once the plant is dormant, late autumn or winter.
BLOOM TIME May/June in temperate gardens. Will rebloom if deadheaded (for those not collecting seed).
LANDSCAPE USE Excellent as a front-of-the-border herbaceous perennial but may need some support, such as a peony cage. Also good in shaded gravel gardens. In regions with acidic soil, raise the pH to neutral by applying ground oyster shells or dolomite lime in a circle around, but not covering, the crown. Prone to late summer mildew (even in the wild).
ZONES 3–11

Clematis 'Alba Luxurians'

Viticella Group, deciduous vine

The prevalence of green markings or tips on the early, cool-weather blossoms of this hybrid put some people who want a true white flower off, but others of us, who appreciate the distinctive look of flowers not quite ripe, are charmed rather than bothered. The stamens are dark. Once the nights get warm, this vigorous vine will whiten its loosely open bell-shaped flowers.

HEIGHT 9–12 feet (3–3.5 m)
LIGHT EXPOSURE Mid- to full sun; especially fine in hot afternoon sun. Shaded roots preferred, but with enough water, it will tolerate sun from the ground up.

PRUNING Hard prune to 1 foot (30 cm) in late winter.
BLOOM TIME After hard pruning in winter, flowers in July/August. This plant responds well to manipulation of standard pruning advice. If pruned by one-half its length after the first wave of bloom, it will rebloom from autumn to frost in temperate climates.
LANDSCAPE USE Excellent at knitting shrub roses together, or loosely covering old-fashioned wire farm fencing. Terrific blending with its kind, or late-flowering large-flowered hybrids.
ZONES 3–11

Clematis alpina 'Pamela Jackman'

Atragene Group, deciduous vine

Although the individual blossoms are not large, this clematis is easily capable of covering its foliage with flowers. Like so many in this group, it has the ability to rebloom in August (or earlier) with a dollop of fertilizer after the first spring performance. The flowers are single, with white stamens and mid-blue sepals that open from bell to flat or even slightly reflexed on a warm spring day.

HEIGHT 9–12 feet (3–3.5 m)
LIGHT EXPOSURE Mid- to full sun. Shaded roots preferred, and gravel rather than organic mulch.
PRUNING Prune as needed after the first wave of blooms is spent, giving the vine the remainder of the growing season to recover. In areas with very cold winters, do not remove the old leaves as they curl around the nodes. This is probably an adaptation to the cold, protecting the latent buds in the node for the coming year.
BLOOM TIME Mid-April through mid-May with good rebloom in 60–90 days.
LANDSCAPE USE Excellent as a pillar, in lilacs and rhododendrons, on fences, decorating evergreen hedges.
ZONES 3–8

Clematis alpina 'Stolwijk Gold'

Atragene Group, deciduous vine

The blue single flowers are pretty enough, I grant you, but the delicate foliage of this clematis serves as the main event. In full sun, it is vivid gold, turning more slightly chartreuse as the growing season progresses. This makes a perfect foil not just for its flowers but for any dynamic blue or purple shorter-growing clematis you may plant in front of it. Or other kinds of flowers, too! So few clematis have a flashy foliage effect, so we all get a little crazy when one does.

HEIGHT 9–12 feet (3–3.5 m)
LIGHT EXPOSURE Mid- to full sun. Shaded roots preferred.
PRUNING Rarely hard pruned, as the foliage effect takes too long to recover. Prune by half immediately after the first wave of flowers in April, if needed, or just remove any winter damage at that time. In areas with very cold winters, do not remove the old leaves as they curl around the nodes. This is probably an adaptation to the cold, protecting the latent buds in the node for the coming year.
BLOOM TIME First wave of blooms in April/May, with modest random rebloom.
LANDSCAPE USE This vine makes an excellent column on a post that has been wrapped with fencing cloth. If allowed to spread out and get tall, it makes a super background for complementary-colored plants.
ZONES 3–8

Clematis 'Anita'

Tangutica/Orientalis Group, deciduous vine

This interesting cross has clean white open bells produced in great masses over a very long season. Even with hard winter pruning, this vine can start flowering in late May and carry on until autumn in temperate climates. The seedheads are silky, as one expects from this group; the difference here is that seed production does not preclude ample continuation of the flowers. Great vigor without much in the way of pesky seedlings.

HEIGHT 12–15 feet (3.5–4.5 m)
LIGHT EXPOSURE Mid- to full sun; especially fine in hot afternoon sun. Shaded roots preferred, but with enough water, it will tolerate sun from the ground up.
PRUNING Hard prune to 1 foot (30 cm) in late winter.
BLOOM TIME After hard pruning in winter, flowers begin in May/June and continue without much encouragement. If flowering flags in hot weather, water more frequently and give a taste of fertilizer.
LANDSCAPE USE This vine makes a superior column on a post that has been wrapped with fencing cloth. Also suitable for creating seasonal shade on an arbor or gazebo. It partners well with the biggest rambling and shrub roses and can also be grown to great effect in conifers that will tolerate a bit of summer companionship.
ZONES 4–10

Clematis 'Aotearoa'

Viticella Group, deciduous vine

The name is the Maori word for New Zealand, "Land of the Long White Cloud." You might think from the translation this might be white-flowering, but think again. Breeder Alister Keay is adept at creating rich dark colors, and 'Aotearoa' may be one of his best. If rich dark red flowers, produced in a long tide of midsummer bounty, is your thing, you will be hard put to find a better doer. Also, this cultivar is very free with new stems, and dividing every 2–3 years will yield many new plants if you want to spread it around. Pronunciation: ay-oh-tee-ah-row-ah, with no accented syllable.

HEIGHT 9–12 feet (3–3.5 m)
LIGHT EXPOSURE Mid- to full sun; especially fine in hot afternoon sun. Shaded roots preferred, but with enough water, it will tolerate sun from the ground up.
PRUNING Hard prune to 1 foot (30 cm) in late winter.
BLOOM TIME After hard pruning in winter, flowers in July/August. This plant responds well to manipulation of standard pruning advice. If pruned by one-half its length after the first wave of bloom, it will rebloom from autumn to frost in temperate climates.
LANDSCAPE USE This dark color is best seen up in the air, in the high arches of a pergola, or in an established variegated small tree, such as *Cornus controversa* 'Variegata' or a variegated box elder.
ZONES 3–11

Clematis 'Apple Blossom'

Evergreen Group, evergreen vine

This hybrid is the most colorful, commonly available version of the cultivars associated with *Clematis armandii*. The shiny dark leaves are more plump than the scimitar-shaped leaves of the species and whiter forms. The fragrance is perhaps a bit lighter but still lovely, carried on a spring breeze. The buds are nearly red, and the sepal reverse holds this color as the blossoms open in their massive trusses. The resemblance to apple blossoms is uncanny.

HEIGHT 20–40 feet (6–12 m)
LIGHT EXPOSURE Mid- to full sun. The vine will shade itself, causing lower leaves to drop, after they blacken. Remove these unsightly leaves, as they hang on longer than you'd like.
PRUNING Prune to whatever degree necessary, in late May after flowering. This gives the plant the growing season to recover enough to flower on time the next year.
BLOOM TIME March/April.
LANDSCAPE USE Everyone wants a fragrant evergreen vine for privacy, or next to the front door. What could possibly go wrong? Keep in mind this is a quick-growing heavy vine. It needs ample support. In the lower reaches of its hardiness range, careful siting is required, or late frosts will rob you of the year's one flush of blooms. Dry cold winter wind will render this "ever-black," and the crisped leaves will hang on like grim death, defacing the new growth with a reminder of winters past.
ZONES 7–11

Clematis 'Arabella'

Integrifolia Group, herbaceous perennial

'Arabella' is an exceptionally popular herbaceous perennial clematis, with good reason. The color after opening is a deep sky blue, which lightens over time. The plant will be leggy if grown in too much shade and is a poor choice for pots, as it will flop and expose bare woody lower stems. In the ground, it is free-flowering over a long season, with ample rebloom if deadheaded or hard pruned in mid-July.

HEIGHT 30–60 inches (0.75–1.5 m)
LIGHT EXPOSURE Minimum six hours of sun daily, tolerates hot western exposures well with sufficient moisture.
PRUNING Reduce to 2 inches (5 cm) once the plant is dormant, late autumn or winter. Deadheading or hard pruning after the first wave of bloom exhausts itself will produce another wave of blooms on shorter stems, often in September/October.
BLOOM TIME May/July in temperate gardens. Will rebloom 30–45 days later if deadheaded.
LANDSCAPE USE Excellent as a mid-border herbaceous perennial but may need a peony cage or some such support. Very effective leaning into roses, weigelas, hydrangeas, and most any deciduous shrub you'd include in a mixed border. This type of clematis can also be used as a groundcover, if planted so that expanding plants will intertwine to cover each other's crowns.
ZONES 4–9

Clematis armandii 'Snowdrift'

Evergreen Group, evergreen vine

This might be the most fragrant selection of *Clematis armandii*. As with others in this group it will be extremely robust in its climate range. The individual white florets may be borne in large trusses, and the fragrance is strong (even overwhelming in an enclosed space). The leaves are scimitar-shaped (more or less), dark and shiny, with grooved veins. In the lower end of its limited hardiness range, the March/April flowers may be lost to a late severe frost.

HEIGHT 20–40 feet (6–12 m)
LIGHT EXPOSURE Full sun, six hours a day or more.
PRUNING Prune as little or as much as needed immediately after flowering. Also, tip prune new growth to keep bushier (assuming you can reach it).
BLOOM TIME March to April. No rebloom.
LANDSCAPE USE Excellent for privacy, or to cover large unsightly structures. Makes too heavy a vine for most living hosts. Site out of cold dry winter wind.
ZONES 8–11

Clematis ×aromatica

Flammula Group, herbaceous perennial

It can arguably be said the French were the most adventurous of clematis breeders of the 1800s. While the English were pumping out large-flowered hybrids, the French were experimenting with small-flowered species. In the present case, the fragrant *Clematis flammula*, native to Europe, was the one parent of which we can be certain. It has been conjectured the other parent was *C. viticella*, but given that both species climb and *C. ×aromatica* does not, this seems unlikely. The more likely pollen or seed parent is *C. integrifolia*. This would contribute the violet-blue color, strengthen the fragrance, and inhibit the ability to climb. The result is *C. ×aromatica*, a floppy thing with an enchanting scent and profusely flowering twee little blossoms composed of four narrow twisting sepals.

HEIGHT 5–6.5 feet (1.5–2 m)

LIGHT EXPOSURE Full sun, six hours a day or more.

PRUNING Since this is an herbaceous perennial, hard pruning down to a few inches tall after dormancy in late autumn or winter is a necessity. All new growth comes from the base.

BLOOM TIME May and June. Cut back by half its length after flowering (or hard prune again) to spur a second flowering in late summer, usually from late August into the autumn.

LANDSCAPE USE Rambles vigorously through other herbaceous perennials; especially good with *Geranium* Rozanne 'Gerwat' and other large mounding hardy geraniums. Leans handsomely into medium to large shrub roses.

ZONES 4–9

Clematis Avant-Garde 'Evipo033'

Viticella Group, deciduous vine

It is always such a delight when a new clematis, something totally distinct, enters the marketplace. Good eye, Raymond Evison, for spotting and propagating this sport of 'Kermesina'. The flowers are small and in every way like 'Kermesina', except for the beguiling tuft of pale pink staminode sepals in the center. Amidst the endless, mind-numbing march of new but undistinguished large-flowered hybrids, a small-flowered form with this much impact in the garden is worth a rousing cheer.

HEIGHT 9–12 feet (3–3.5 m)
LIGHT EXPOSURE Mid- to full sun.
PRUNING Hard prune to 1 foot (30 cm) in late winter.
BLOOM TIME After hard pruning in winter, flowers in July/ August. This plant responds well to manipulation of standard pruning advice. If pruned by one-half its length after the first wave of bloom, it will rebloom from autumn to frost in temperate climates. The volume of bloom is breathtaking.
LANDSCAPE USE There is a certain festivity about this plant that should be exploited for all it's worth. Give it a wire fence to decorate, or a medium to dark green broadleaf evergreen or conifer to set off the fluffy little center amidst the hot red of the outer sepals. Think filigree.
ZONES 3–11

Clematis 'Bells of Emei Shan'

semi-evergreen groundcover

Plantsman Dan Hinkley found this creeping groundcover clematis growing in a rain forest on Mount Emei Shan in China. Because it is not *exactly* like *Clematis repens*, the taxonomical "splitters" had their way, and Dan gave it a cultivar name in 2006. At that time, the plant and its seeds were widely circulated amongst clematis cognoscenti, who called it by Dan's collection number, 795. Hence, one may hear this plant spoken of by the cultivar name, as *C. repens*, or simply as "795." The thick, waxy yellow bell-shaped flowers are produced all summer on thin vines with leathery leaves. It can climb, sort of, but is better at grabbing hold of itself, forming dreadlocks. Slightly fragrant.

HEIGHT 4 feet (1.2 m) or less
LIGHT EXPOSURE Must have partial to dense shade, and absolutely no hot afternoon sun.
PRUNING In mid-spring, maybe April or so, prune away any dieback from the winter, and watch the crown and stems for new growth.
BLOOM TIME Late May through June and longer, especially if deadheaded. If grown in a container where its draping habit can be admired, a tomato fertilizer application in midsummer may bring on more blooms.
LANDSCAPE USE This is truly a shade-loving groundcover. Ideal with ferns in mossy environments. In containers, mulch with moss. It was found in the wild growing under and over a nurse log, so it is ideal for stumperies under old rhododendrons.
ZONES 7–9

Clematis 'Betty Corning'

Viticella Group, deciduous vine

So far, this is the only hybrid of the water-loving *Clematis crispa* to be widely available. Its other parent (we presume) is *C. viticella*, and this imparts a larger, pagoda-roof blossom and staggering vigor. A mature, well-grown clump will produce dozens and dozens of vining stems. From *C. crispa* comes the delectable scent, soft lavender-blue color, and tolerance for wet feet; constantly damp soil is no problem. Beware of buying seed-grown plants: they may lack scent. Seek divisions and cutting-grown plants from well-scented clones.

HEIGHT to 10 feet (3 m) and as wide at the top
LIGHT EXPOSURE Mid- to full sun; shaded roots preferred.
PRUNING Hard prune to 1 foot (30 cm) in late winter.
BLOOM TIME After hard pruning in winter, flowers in July/August. This plant responds well to manipulation of standard pruning advice. If pruned by one-half its length after the first wave of bloom, it will rebloom from autumn to frost in temperate climates.
LANDSCAPE USE Place where the scent can be appreciated. Although the plant might become massive, the individual canes are lightweight. Excellent in large shrubs and small trees.
ZONES 3–9

Clematis 'Bill MacKenzie' ✽

Tangutica/Orientalis Group, deciduous vine

The true form of this vine was nearly lost to the American trade due to the persistence of suppliers growing it from seed. When you grow plants from hybrid seed, you rarely get the original. Thankfully, nurseryman David Mason went back to Waterperry Gardens where the plant originated, and was allowed to take fresh cuttings to ensure true stock. Many consider this the best cultivar in the Tangutica/Orientalis Group, and it would be a shame to lose it due to negligence. Its yellow lantern flowers are larger than most in this group, the length of the bloom period is outstanding, and the centers are usually, but not always (even on the same plant), dark.

HEIGHT 13–16.5 feet (4–5 m)

LIGHT EXPOSURE Mid- to full sun; especially fine in hot afternoon sun. With enough water, it will tolerate sun from the ground up.

PRUNING Hard prune to 1 foot (30 cm) in late winter.

BLOOM TIME After hard pruning in winter, flowers begin in early June, and continue without much encouragement. If flowering flags in hot weather, water more frequently and give a taste of fertilizer.

LANDSCAPE USE In the UK this is often seen in public gardens paired with 'Étoile Violette'. Do give it a sturdy structure or a mature woody plant host to climb, even though you'll cut it back hard every winter. He's a bruiser, is our "Bill."

ZONES 4–9

Clematis 'Blekitny Aniol' Blue Angel

Viticella Group, deciduous vine

The trade name here is a direct translation of the Polish. We sometimes see this listed as a late large-flowered hybrid, but the growth habit, style of blossom, and foliage clearly proclaim the heritage. The color is indeed an angelic lavender-blue, and the vigor further attests to *Clematis viticella*, or some form of it, in the parentage.

HEIGHT 10–14 feet (3–4 m)
LIGHT EXPOSURE Mid- to full sun; especially fine in hot afternoon sun. Shaded roots preferred, but with enough water, it will tolerate sun from the ground up.

PRUNING Hard prune to 1 foot (30 cm) in late winter.
BLOOM TIME After hard pruning in winter, flowers in July/August. This plant responds well to manipulation of standard pruning advice. If pruned by one-half its length after the first wave of bloom, it will rebloom from autumn to frost in temperate climates.
LANDSCAPE USE Excellent on arbors consorting with pastel pink or yellow climbing roses; also a good companion for dwarf fruit trees (plant at the drip line of the tree).
ZONES 4–9

Clematis 'Blue Belle'
Viticella Group, deciduous vine

Tall, dark, and handsome, that's 'Blue Belle', even though the name implies femininity—and another color altogether. This is a robust climber with truly luscious purple blossoms. The bright creamy boss of stamens enlivens the dark color, making the plant easier to place. This classic is just one of the many introductions by Ernest Markham, head gardener for William Robinson of Gravetye Manor.

HEIGHT 10–14 feet (3–4 m)

LIGHT EXPOSURE Mid- to full sun; especially fine in hot afternoon sun. Shaded roots preferred, but with enough water, it will tolerate sun from the ground up.

PRUNING Hard prune to 1 foot (30 cm) in late winter.

BLOOM TIME After hard pruning in winter, flowers in July/August. This plant responds well to manipulation of standard pruning advice. If pruned by one-half its length after the first wave of bloom, it will rebloom from autumn to frost in temperate climates.

LANDSCAPE USE Excellent planted in combination with other, lighter-colored clematis. If you are putting different forms of *Clematis viticella* on each post of a pergola, include this as the darkest hybrid.

ZONES 3–9

Clematis 'Bluebird'

Atragene Group, deciduous vine

This is a fluffy light blue ballet-skirt of a flower. The vine's vigor is excellent, as is its ability to rebloom, and as one of Frank Skinner's introductions, you know it is bone-hardy. Since he was working in the short-season climate of Canada, Skinner probably never realized how reliably this clematis would rebloom in the long growing seasons of zones 7 and 8.

HEIGHT 6.5–13 feet (2–4 m)
LIGHT EXPOSURE Mid- to full sun. Shaded roots preferred, and gravel rather than organic mulch.

PRUNING Prune as needed after the first wave of blooms is spent, giving the vine the remainder of the growing season to recover. In areas with very cold winters, do not remove the old leaves as they curl around the nodes. This is probably an adaptation to the cold, protecting the latent buds in the node for the coming year.
BLOOM TIME Mid-April through mid-May with good rebloom in 60–90 days.
LANDSCAPE USE Excellent as a pillar, and effective for adding interest to broadleaf evergreen hedges. Very pretty flowering amongst the white bracts of *Viburnum plicatum* f. *tomentosum* 'Mariesii', and the clematis will then decorate the doublefile viburnum a second time, later in the summer.
ZONES 3–9

Clematis 'Blue Dancer'
Atragene Group, deciduous vine

The flowers of 'Blue Dancer' have been likened to wind-socks, and while they are not *that* big, these are the longest sepals of any flower in this group. The blue is sapphire-like in its depth, and the extra length makes the blossoms bob and nod cheerfully in a spring breeze. No one knows quite how it happened, but an error on some plant tag somewhere led to the confusion of this cultivar with the smaller-flowered but equally blue 'Frances Rivis', known for its white, spatulate (spoonlike) staminodes.

HEIGHT 6.5–10 feet (2–3 m)
LIGHT EXPOSURE Mid- to full sun. Shaded roots preferred, and gravel rather than organic mulch.
PRUNING Prune as needed after the first wave of blooms is spent, giving the vine the remainder of the growing season to recover. In areas with very cold winters, do not remove the old leaves as they curl around the nodes. This is probably an adaptation to the cold, protecting the latent buds in the node for the coming year.
BLOOM TIME Mid-April through mid-May with good rebloom in 60–90 days.
LANDSCAPE USE Excellent as a pillar, in deciduous or evergreen hedges, and on fences as a backdrop for spring ephemerals, both herbaceous perennials and bulbs.
ZONES 3–9

Clematis Bonanza 'Evipo031'
Viticella Group, deciduous vine

Although the parentage of this vigorous and cheerful hybrid has not yet been revealed, everything about it screams Viticella Group. The color is bright lavender, often with a creamy paler bar, which makes the color pop. The flowers are profuse and in full sun will cover the vine from the ground up.

HEIGHT 9–10.5 feet (3 m)
LIGHT EXPOSURE Mid- to full sun; especially fine in hot afternoon sun. Shaded roots preferred, but with enough water, it will tolerate sun from the ground up.
PRUNING Hard prune to 1 foot (30 cm) in late winter.
BLOOM TIME After hard pruning in winter, flowers in July/August. This plant responds well to manipulation of standard pruning advice. If pruned by one-half its length after the first wave of bloom, it will rebloom from autumn to frost in temperate climates.
LANDSCAPE USE Very effective on a flat-panel trellis as a backdrop for herbaceous perennials in yellows, peach, and cream. This vine combines well with shorter plants for quite painterly effects.
ZONES 4–9

Clematis 'Broughton Star'

Montana Group, deciduous vine

This cultivar is an improvement on 'Marjorie', the only other previously common double form of *Clematis montana*, one of this vine's parents. Here we have an increased depth of pink color, and more substance to both the outer and staminode sepals. Like most in this group, the mature size might give most gardeners pause (whether feet or meters, its listed height is a staggering underestimation), but if you have room for only one representative of the Montana Group, this is an excellent choice.

HEIGHT 16.5–23 feet (5–7 m)

LIGHT EXPOSURE Mid- to full sun. If planted in partial shade, the plant will seek the amount of sun it requires to bloom well.

PRUNING Prune to whatever degree necessary in late June, after flowering. This gives the plant the growing season to recover enough to flower on time the next year. Many in the Montana Group benefit from a rejuvenating hard pruning every 3–5 years.

BLOOM TIME March/April.

LANDSCAPE USE Useful wherever a large showy vine is wanted. The flowers impress by their color and volume, not by the size of individual blossoms. Most cultivars in this group become large and quite heavy-trunked over time—plan accordingly for ample support. The fragrance of the double Montana Group forms is not so strong as that of the single forms, but the flowers last longer.

ZONES 7–10

Clematis 'Brunette'

Atragene Group, deciduous vine

Of all those in the garden-worthy Atragene Group, this gets my vote as most likely to succeed in a large container with good drainage. It will not want to share its bunk with other plants, so no allowing annuals and weeds to horn in. The puce (purple/brown) or even mahogany flowers commence blooming in April and continue off and on all summer. The rebloom is more pronounced when plants get a taste of any sort of blossom-booster or tomato fertilizer every few weeks, if grown in a pot. In the ground, such attention is not necessary.

HEIGHT 7–10 feet (2–3 m)

LIGHT EXPOSURE Mid- to full sun. Shaded roots preferred, and gravel rather than organic mulch.

PRUNING Prune as needed after the first wave of blooms is spent, giving the vine the remainder of the growing season to recover. In areas with very cold winters, do not remove the old leaves as they curl around the nodes. This is probably an adaptation to the cold, protecting the latent buds in the node for the coming year.

BLOOM TIME Mid-April through mid-May with good rebloom throughout the growing season.

LANDSCAPE USE Excellent in containers, where the dark color can be appreciated up close. Also effective in hydrangeas, especially the white mopheads.

ZONES 3–9

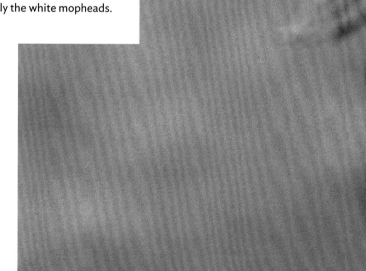

Clematis 'Carmencita'
Viticella Group, deciduous vine

Some of the best red flowers in the genus are found in the Viticella Group, and 'Carmencita' should be included in anyone's top five reds. Breeder Magnus Johnson dubbed this his "dark-eyed Spanish beauty," and one can easily imagine a fiery Latin dancer wearing this color. The sepals have a more velvety surface than most in this group, and the intensity of color is deeper at the margins.

HEIGHT 10–14 feet (3–4 m)
LIGHT EXPOSURE Mid- to full sun; especially fine in hot afternoon sun.
PRUNING Hard prune to 1 foot (30 cm) in late winter.
BLOOM TIME After hard pruning in winter, flowers in July/August. This plant responds well to manipulation of standard pruning advice. If pruned by one-half its length after the first wave of bloom, it will rebloom from autumn to frost in temperate climates.
LANDSCAPE USE Use where a red vine is needed. This is a plant with the courage of its convictions: the color is unfading, and the growth is robust enough to compete with other vines (honeysuckles, hops, solanums) as long as roots are widely spaced.
ZONES 4–10

Clematis ×*cartmanii* 'Joe'
Evergreen Group, evergreen non-clinging vine

The hybrids derived from New Zealand species can be a bit of a trick to grow if you don't live in New Zealand, but their unique foliage—like stiff parsley—and their clean white March flowers make them well worth the effort. In most climates, the issue is drainage, not cold. The best specimens of this plant I have seen were either in troughs or in raised beds with 50% gravel worked into the soil. This is a cross between the world's smallest *Clematis* species, *C. marmoraria* (a subalpine shrublet, to 8 inches/20 cm tall and wide), and a big rambling vine, *C. paniculata* (to 15 feet/4.5 m). The combination yields an evergreen to semi-evergreen non-climber. Prefers soil with a higher pH.

HEIGHT 4–6.5 feet (1.2–2 m)
LIGHT EXPOSURE Mid- to full sun, but needs shaded roots.
PRUNING Prune to whatever degree necessary in early May, after flowering. This gives the plant the growing season to recover enough to flower on time the next year.
BLOOM TIME March/April.
LANDSCAPE USE Excellent in troughs or large containers where drainage and pH can be well controlled. In a raised gravel bed, this tries to clamber up any surrounding shrubs, but it does not truly grab hold, so fasten with Velcro if you want it to be vertical.
ZONES 7–9

Clematis 'Cecile'

Atragene Group, deciduous vine

This hybrid involving *Clematis macropetala* distinguishes itself from the other excellent blues in this group by being one of the earliest to bloom. In the race to flower, 'Cecile' will open with the first warm day in late March, assuming there is one. The color is lovely, and light violet veining lends the sepals unusual detailing.

HEIGHT 7–9 feet (2–3 m)

LIGHT EXPOSURE Mid- to full sun. Shaded roots preferred, and gravel rather than organic mulch.

PRUNING Prune as needed after the first wave of blooms is spent, giving the vine the remainder of the growing season to recover. In areas with very cold winters, do not remove the old leaves as they curl around the nodes. This is probably an adaptation to the cold, protecting the latent buds in the node for the coming year.

BLOOM TIME Mid-April through mid-May with good rebloom in 60–90 days.

LANDSCAPE USE Tolerates life in a container better than most. Excellent on a flat-panel trellis, where it will make a thrilling display with excellent rebloom in August where summers are warm enough to ripen the new wood.

ZONES 3–9

Clematis chiisanensis 'Lemon Bells'

Atragene Group, deciduous vine

Clematis chiisanensis is from South Korea and is thought by some to be identical to *C. koreana* var. *lutea*. The UBC Botanical Garden made their selection from wild-collected seed. 'Lemon Bells' is distinguished from the type by having a beguiling dusting of cinnamon on its "shoulder-pads" (to quote clematis expert Mary Toomey). The flowers are indeed lemon yellow. *Clematis chiisanensis* and to a lesser extent *C. koreana* have detectable spurs on their sepals, proving their relation to many other genera in the Ranunculaceae.

HEIGHT 7–10 feet (2–3 m)
LIGHT EXPOSURE Mid- to full sun. Shaded roots preferred, and gravel rather than organic mulch. Tolerates some shade.

PRUNING Prune as needed after the first wave of blooms is spent, giving the vine the remainder of the growing season to recover. In areas with very cold winters, do not remove the old leaves as they curl around the nodes. This is probably an adaptation to the cold, protecting the latent buds in the node for the coming year.
BLOOM TIME Mid-April through mid-June with good rebloom in 60–90 days, once the new growth ripens in long-season climates.
LANDSCAPE USE Excellent as a pillar or on arbors and fences, and it drapes beautifully down a retaining wall.
ZONES 4–9

Clematis cirrhosa var. balearica

Cirrhosa Group, semi-evergreen/evergreen vine

This variety of *Clematis cirrhosa* is from the Balearic Islands, specifically Minorca. The foliage, ferny and delicate, is my favorite of the genus. It has a tendency to go bronze in cold winter weather, which highlights the handsome little bells, which are creamy with red spots or streaks.

HEIGHT 9–16.5 feet (3–5 m)
LIGHT EXPOSURE Mid- to full sun. If planted in partial shade, the plant will seek the amount of sun it requires to bloom well. Handles hot afternoon sun beautifully.
PRUNING Prune to whatever degree necessary in May or June. This gives the plant the growing season to recover enough to flower on time the next year. If the plant loses its leaves, it will likely be in summer. Don't let a month or two of summer dormancy scare you. Do hard prune every 3–4 years to rejuvenate the base of the plant.
BLOOM TIME November through March.
LANDSCAPE USE One plant is sufficient to fill a trellis 8 feet (2.5 m) tall and half as wide. This makes a bigger vine than the others in this group, so plan accordingly.
ZONES 7–9

Clematis cirrhosa 'Ourika Valley'

Cirrhosa Group, semi-evergreen/evergreen vine

The Cirrhosa Group are winter-flowering, blooming from October/November through March in happy circumstances. These need at least a half day of sun and great drainage to do well in temperate wet climates, but they are much hardier than given credit for. This particular selection has bell-shaped flowers more yellow than the type, and no streaks of burgundy. Vigorous.

HEIGHT 9–13 feet (3–4 m)
LIGHT EXPOSURE Mid- to full sun. If planted in partial shade, the plant will seek the amount of sun it requires to bloom well.
PRUNING Prune to whatever degree necessary in May or June. This gives the plant the growing season to recover enough to flower on time the next year. If the plant loses its leaves, it will likely be in summer. Don't let a month or two of summer dormancy scare you. Do hard prune every 3–4 years to rejuvenate the base of the plant.
BLOOM TIME October through March, off and on.
LANDSCAPE USE One plant is sufficient to fill a trellis 8 feet (2.5 m) tall and half as wide. Also effective in big deciduous shrubs—when the shrub (say, for instance, a big viburnum) loses its leaves, voila! a winter-blooming clematis is revealed!
ZONES 7–9

Clematis cirrhosa var. *purpurascens* 'Freckles'

Cirrhosa Group, evergreen/ semi-evergreen vine

'Freckles' is a delight, producing its cheery freckled and splashed bells from November through March. Bouts of severe cold may stop it momentarily, but in zones 7–9 it will bounce back and resume flowering in less than 30 days. Here the characteristic bells are ornamented with bright to dark red streaks. In some selections made from 'Freckles', the specks are so thickly peppered that the sepals appear lined with solid red. All these further selections are unstable: they do not consistently produce all-red flowers. But 'Freckles' is always a safe bet.

HEIGHT 13–16.5 feet (4–5 m)
LIGHT EXPOSURE Mid- to full sun. If planted in partial shade, the plant will seek the amount of sun it requires to bloom well.
PRUNING Prune to whatever degree is necessary in May or June. This gives the plant the growing season to recover enough to flower on time the next year. If the plant loses its leaves, it will likely happen in summer. Don't let a month or two of summer dormancy scare you. Do hard prune every 3–4 years to rejuvenate the base of the plant.
BLOOM TIME October through March, off and on.
LANDSCAPE USE One plant is sufficient to fill a trellis 8 feet (2.5 m) tall and half as wide. Great fun to use as drapery on retaining walls, or in winter-interest conifer gardens. Be careful, though. Not all conifers take well to being upholstered by clematis.
ZONES 7–9

Clematis 'Clochette Pride'

Atragene Group, deciduous vine

The original name of this hybrid, 'Campanulina Plena' (Latin for "double-belled flower"), was disallowed by the International Code of Nomenclature just when everyone had learned to pronounce it. The new name bestowed by its creator, Magnus Johnson of Sweden, does not come any more trippingly to the tongue. No matter—if I could choose but one from the Atragene Group, this would be it. These fully double flowers are luscious deep violet, and the vines are exceptionally free-flowering. It is also quite a stud, giving rise to handsome seedlings that are always worth a look before being consigned to the compost heap.

HEIGHT 6.5–10 feet (2–3 m)
LIGHT EXPOSURE Mid- to full sun. Shaded roots preferred, and gravel rather than organic mulch.
PRUNING Prune as needed after the first wave of blooms is spent, giving the vine the remainder of the growing season to recover. In areas with very cold winters, do not remove the old leaves as they curl around the nodes. This is probably an adaptation to the cold, protecting the latent buds in the node for the coming year.
BLOOM TIME Mid-April through mid-May with excellent rebloom in 60–90 days.
LANDSCAPE USE The dark flowers require careful placement. Best in gray-foliaged or variegated plants.
ZONES 3–8

Clematis 'Constance' ❖

Atragene Group, deciduous vine

Although the flowers are not as richly colored as those of parent 'Ruby', their shade of dark violet-pink is carrying and pretty. This selection is one of the earliest to flower: think of March as a three-way race in this group between 'Cecile', 'Constance', and 'Jan Lindmark', with 'Constance' a consistent favorite for the profusion and frequency of its blooms.

HEIGHT 6.5–13 feet (2–4 m)

LIGHT EXPOSURE Mid- to full sun. Shaded roots preferred, and gravel rather than organic mulch.

PRUNING Prune as needed after the first wave of blooms is spent, giving the vine the remainder of the growing season to recover. In areas with very cold winters, do not remove the old leaves as they curl around the nodes. This is probably an adaptation to the cold, protecting the latent buds in the node for the coming year.

BLOOM TIME Late March through late April with ample rebloom in 60 days.

LANDSCAPE USE Best used to add color to out-of-bloom shrubs such as witch hazel (*Hamamelis*) or winter-flowering viburnums.

ZONES 3–8

Clematis crispa

herbaceous vine

This is a favorite species for numerous reasons. It is fragrant, which is a characteristic passed along to any of its hybrids. For this reason, and its love of water, it is known locally as "the swamp hyacinth" in the southeastern United States. It must have wet soil, the boggier the better. It has a long period of bloom, June through mid-autumn, and the bell-shaped blossoms are curly in every way. The pale to dark lavender sepals flip back at their tips, often making a 360° ringlet. The sepal edges are wavy as a crinoline petticoat. The seedheads are huge, and the tails stay spiky, never fluffing out like feathers. The vine is lightweight.

HEIGHT 4–10 feet (1.2–3 m)

LIGHT EXPOSURE Partial shade preferred, but tolerates full sun if its feet are constantly wet. Not moist, *wet*.

PRUNING Hard prune in the winter or early spring. There is little rejuvenation of the upper vines, and it is better to let the whole thing start over every year.

BLOOM TIME June through late September, continuous without deadheading.

LANDSCAPE USE Combine *Clematis crispa* with other water-loving plants such as hydrangeas. For flower texture contrast at its very best, set these curly bells amongst lacecap and woodland hydrangeas.

ZONES 5–10

Clematis 'Dark Dancer'

Atragene Group, deciduous vine

I was privileged to see this seedling mature in the display gardens at Joy Creek Nursery in Scappoose, Oregon. Imagine a dark purple 'Blue Dancer', bouncing just as easily in the spring breezes, and you have a fair idea of how attractive this cultivar is. Would that every volunteer clematis seedling was born with such charms. In areas with cool spring nights and overcast days, the color stays very dark.

HEIGHT 6–7 feet (1.8–2 m)

LIGHT EXPOSURE Mid- to full sun. Shaded roots preferred, and gravel rather than organic mulch.

PRUNING Prune as needed after the first wave of blooms is spent, giving the vine the remainder of the growing season to recover. In areas with very cold winters, do not remove the old leaves as they curl around the nodes. This is probably an adaptation to the cold, protecting the latent buds in the node for the coming year.

BLOOM TIME Mid-April through mid-May with good rebloom in 60–90 days.

LANDSCAPE USE Excellent as a pillar and on gray-foliaged shrubs. Also very handsome in selections of *Tsuga canadensis* with white new growth, such as 'Gentsch White' and 'Summer Snow'.

ZONES 3–8

Clematis 'Dark Eyes'

Viticella Group, deciduous vine

This 2006 German introduction is fast winning a place amongst the first ranks of Viticella Group hybrids. The color is as dark a purple as one would imagine given the name. The boss of stamens lends fascination, as the filaments are persistently light green, the pollen nearly white, and the connectives holding the two anthers together almost black. The intriguing center gives this plant its distinction above the endless ranks of dark-flowered viticellas.

HEIGHT Breeder says 5–7 feet (1.5–2 m), but I have seen it much taller at Joy Creek Nursery's display garden, to perhaps 12 feet (3.5 m).

LIGHT EXPOSURE Mid- to full sun; especially fine in hot afternoon sun. Shaded roots preferred.

PRUNING Hard prune to 1 foot (30 cm) in late winter.

BLOOM TIME After hard pruning in winter, flowers in July/August. This plant responds well to manipulation of standard pruning advice. If pruned by one-half its length after the first wave of bloom, it will rebloom from autumn to frost in temperate climates.

LANDSCAPE USE Best used on high arches or in taller trees where the dark flowers swagging along would be most visible.

ZONES 3–11

Clematis ×*diversifolia* 'Heather Herschell' ✤

Integrifolia Group, herbaceous perennial

Once upon a time, in the 1830s, *Clematis integrifolia* and *C. viticella* were crossed, most likely with *C. integrifolia* as the seed—and thus more influential—parent. The exact result, which is no longer with us, was a big, floppy, non-climbing herbaceous perennial, with open, pagoda-roof flowers in some shade of purple, blue, or pinkish lavender. In the present case, the exact parentage is not known, but presumably a pink *C. integrifolia* cultivar (perhaps the selection 'Rosea' or the hybrid 'Pangbourne Pink') was the seed parent. The resultant plant is whimsical and free-flowering, producing lovely pink blossoms widened at the sepal tips and twisting like paddles in the air.

HEIGHT 5–6.5 feet (1.5–2 m)

LIGHT EXPOSURE Full sun, six hours a day or more.

PRUNING Since this is an herbaceous perennial, hard pruning down to a few inches tall after dormancy in late autumn or winter is a necessity. All new growth comes from the base.

BLOOM TIME June through August. Cut back by half its length after flowering (or hard prune again) to spur a second flowering in late summer, usually from September into the autumn in shorter stems.

LANDSCAPE USE A good choice for leaning into out-of-bloom forsythias or woodier *Euonymus* forms. Handsome with medium to large shrub roses and hydrangeas.

ZONES 4–9

Clematis 'Duchess of Albany'

Texensis Group, herbaceous vine

As voluminous as a well-grown plant of this cultivar may be, very little of the current season's growth rejuvenates from year to year. The whole replenishes itself annually before flowering away, with an abundance of pink blossoms shaped like lily-flowered tulips. This and 'Sir Trevor Lawrence' are the only remnants of a series of *Clematis texensis* hybrids bred in the 1890s by Jackman's Nursery in Woking—and therefore known as the Wokingensis hybrids. It has been suggested that *all* the *C. texensis* hybrids be so designated, but since the term Wokingensis refers to a particular group of seedlings, only two of which are extant, it makes more sense to refer to both the old and modern hybrids as the Texensis Group.

HEIGHT 6.5–13 feet (2–4 m)

LIGHT EXPOSURE Must have full sun to bloom well, preferably from the ground up. Too much shade produces all vine and leaves with no blossoms.

PRUNING Hard prune in the winter or early spring. There is little rejuvenation of the upper vines; it is better to let the whole thing start over every year.

BLOOM TIME Late June through mid-October, continuous without deadheading.

LANDSCAPE USE Excellent in climbing roses. Someday I'd like to grow this clematis with a stand of *Dahlia* 'Giraffe', which has narrow petals in various sherbet shades with horizontal stripes of darker hues. Also makes an excellent full-sun groundcover.

ZONES 4–9

Clematis ×durandii ✤

Integrifolia Group, herbaceous perennial

If you get ten clematarians in a room and ask for the top ten clematis favorites from each, this clematis will most likely appear on every list. This is another interesting French cross; this time *Clematis integrifolia* mated with one of the founding large-flowered species, *C. lanuginosa*, rarely seen now but highly influential in its day. How influential? *Clematis lanuginosa* is one parent of 'Jackmanii'. In *C. ×durandii*, this large-flowered parent intensified the color to a striking mid-blue, widened the sepals, and gives an out- or upfacing flower, rather than the typical *C. integrifolia* bell. It does not climb.

HEIGHT 3.5–10 feet (1–3 m)
LIGHT EXPOSURE Full sun, six hours a day or more.

PRUNING Since this is an herbaceous perennial, hard pruning down to a few inches tall after dormancy in late autumn or winter is a necessity. All new growth comes from the base.

BLOOM TIME May and June. Cut back by half its length after flowering (or hard prune again) to spur a second flowering in late summer, usually from mid-August into the autumn.

LANDSCAPE USE Leans handsomely into medium to large shrub roses. Flowers of this particular shade of blue pair well with yellow- to cream-variegated foliage, such as *Cotinus coggygria* Golden Spirit 'Ancot', or *Weigela* 'Florida Variegata'.

ZONES 4–9

Clematis 'Emilia Plater' ✿

Viticella Group, deciduous vine

This charming vine, yet another wonderful introduction from Brother Stefan Franczak of Poland, is not as well known as it should be, even with its inclusion in the International Clematis Society's Clematis for Beginners list. Its sepals are more distinctly lavender than blue, a point that is often emphasized by a darker lavender midrib, and it's a very durable, robust grower.

HEIGHT 7–10 feet (2–3 m)
LIGHT EXPOSURE Mid- to full sun; especially fine in hot afternoon sun. Shaded roots preferred, but with enough water, it will tolerate sun from the ground up.
PRUNING Hard prune to 1 foot (30 cm) in late winter.
BLOOM TIME After hard pruning in winter, flowers in July/August. This plant responds well to manipulation of standard pruning advice. If pruned by one-half its length after the first wave of bloom, it will rebloom from autumn to frost in temperate climates.
LANDSCAPE USE Makes a lovely column of itself, staying bushy and ample from the ground up. If you plan to grow it into a large shrub, do give the shrub a running start; plant the clematis at the drip line of the established shrub.
ZONES 4–10

Clematis 'Early Sensation'

Evergreen Group, evergreen non-clinging vine

Like *Clematis* ×*cartmanii* 'Joe', this plant requires good drainage and prefers soil with a higher pH. But it is much more site-adaptable, and although not a secure climber, it can get several feet longer than 'Joe', moving up an open-weave wire trellis with some ease. The flowers are prolifically produced, and the foliage is dark shiny green. Loads of big clean white flowers to 3 inches (7.5 cm) in diameter. Allegedly fragrant, but I have never noticed it.

HEIGHT 6.5–10 feet (2–3 m)
LIGHT EXPOSURE Mid- to full sun.
PRUNING Prune to whatever degree necessary in May or June. This gives the plant the growing season to recover enough to flower on time the next year. Do hard prune every 3–4 years to rejuvenate the base of the plant.
BLOOM TIME March and April, with lovely seedheads in May.
LANDSCAPE USE Very effective running over *Thujopsis dolabrata* 'Nana', bird's nest spruce (*Picea abies* 'Nidiformis'), or similarly shaped conifers. Good in rock gardens and as a groundcover, too.
ZONES 7–9

Clematis 'Étoile Rose'

Viticella Group,
herbaceous vine

The supply of this plant never exceeds the demand, and no wonder, with so much charm and robust ease of care on offer. It also stands to reason it is claimed by more than one horticultural group within the genus, since its pollen parent was *Clematis viticella*, and its mother was half *C. texensis* (which it more closely resembles). If the presence of *C. hirsutissima* var. *scottii* in the genetic mix means the breeders were attempting to create a diminutive creature, they failed. The flowers are rosy reddish on the outside, somewhat shaped like a shorter, chubbier lily-flowered tulip, and the interior has a rosy bar over a pink ground.

HEIGHT 7–9 feet (2–3 m)
LIGHT EXPOSURE Full sun preferred.
PRUNING Hard prune in the winter or early spring. There is little rejuvenation of the upper vines, and it is better to let the whole thing start over every year.
BLOOM TIME July through late September, continuous without deadheading.
LANDSCAPE USE Create lovely texture and color contrast by growing through large shrub roses and such summer-blooming shrubs as *Abelia* ×*grandiflora*.
ZONES 5–10

Clematis 'Étoile Violette' ✤

Viticella Group, deciduous vine

For every person who starts their clematis-growing career with 'Jackmanii', there must be at least as many who start here, with this elegant French antique (1885). It is long-lived, adaptable, and lends itself to unusual uses (such as enhancing Douglas firs). In public gardens, this is consistently combined with 'Bill MacKenzie' or another yellow Tangutica/Orientalis Group form to wonderful effect.

HEIGHT 8–13 feet (2.5–4 m)
LIGHT EXPOSURE Mid- to full sun; especially fine in hot afternoon sun.
PRUNING Hard prune to 1 foot (30 cm) in late winter.
BLOOM TIME After hard pruning in winter, flowers in July/August. This plant responds well to manipulation of standard pruning advice. If pruned by one-half its length after the first wave of bloom, it will rebloom from autumn to frost in temperate climates.
LANDSCAPE USE Excellent combined with roses, and well shown with vines with white flowers. I've seen this growing into *Passiflora caerulea* (blue passionflower) in a Dublin garden and looking quite grand. If *Euonymus fortunei* 'Emerald Gaiety' is allowed to indulge its vining tendencies, 'Étoile Violette' makes a swell partner.
ZONES 3–9

Clematis fasciculiflora
evergreen vine

The problem with most evergreen clematis is their need for full sun. This woodland species from China is quite forgiving in this regard. This late winter/early spring bloomer attracts newly arrived hummingbirds to its creamy bells, another decided advantage. And the third great feature of this clematis is the silver marbling on mature leaves, with occasional bronzing of the new foliage. There isn't a lot of variegation amongst the clematis, so plants like this get the cognoscenti all excited. All in all, a more garden-worthy evergreen vine.

HEIGHT 13–16.5 feet (4–5 m)
LIGHT EXPOSURE Partial shade, especially dappled deciduous shade. Tolerates western exposure only in the winter. Summer afternoon heat makes for crispy foliage.
PRUNING Prune as much or as little as needed after it completes its annual flower cycle in early May.
BLOOM TIME Late February after a warm winter, otherwise March into early May.
LANDSCAPE USE Makes a great "hedge binder" for northern or eastern exposures. Great on residential structures, as it is not invasive or too heavy.
ZONES 7–9, 6 if sheltered

Clematis flammula
deciduous vine

This is the most fragrant of the Flammula Group species, and also quite vigorous, even boisterous, when it is well grown. The small frothy white flowers burst upon our noses in high summer when other fragrant clematis are either long finished (the Montana Group) or not yet started (*Clematis terniflora*). This species is native from the northern shores of the Mediterranean into the steppes of the Middle East. Widely used in breeding to add vigor and fragrance to a seed strain. Folks can be disappointed in *C. flammula* grown from seed, as young plants may take 2–3 years to develop their scent. Patience, people, clematis teach us patience.

HEIGHT 10.5–16.5 feet (3–5 m)
LIGHT EXPOSURE Best with sun from the ground up, all day.
PRUNING Hard prune in the winter or early spring. Flowers best on new growth.
BLOOM TIME Late June through late summer and autumn, until nights get cold.
LANDSCAPE USE Great as a "filler" in gardens; mature plants produce many stems and fling themselves around in multiple directions. Plant this in a moon garden; the flowers take on a luminous silver cast at twilight, and the fragrance is divine at night, with a scent that is lighter than jasmine.
ZONES 4–9

Clematis fremontii
herbaceous perennial

Recent discovery of what are likely the seminal populations in the state of Georgia have us rethinking this species, long thought to be a denizen of midwestern prairies. These new groups are growing in situations and climates that are very different from the prairie tribe, which explains why this is such a good garden plant: it is highly adaptable. The flowers are little lightly fuzzy bells, light purple with greenish margins (more creamy than green in Georgia). The prairie populations are sun-adapted and disperse their seed in tumbleweed fashion. In the Georgia populations, the plants are in deciduous glades in high shade and heavily browsed by deer (quite a different seed-scattering mechanism!). Prefers soil with a higher pH.

HEIGHT 12–24 inches (30–60 cm); the Georgia group is generally taller than the prairie group.
LIGHT EXPOSURE This will depend upon where your seed came from. Prairie-grown plants will want full sun.
PRUNING Do not be alarmed when the leaves of this herbaceous perennial skeletonize in early winter, and the whole thing appears to rot off at ground level without your lifting a finger. It is preparing to roll those seeds around the garden. It will return and flower early the following year.
BLOOM TIME April into May, with repeat if deadheaded. In Georgia, protect from deer. So far, the Georgia populations are being withheld from the market for conservation.
LANDSCAPE USE Use in troughs or rock gardens. Charming when blooming with dwarf shrubs, such as *Berberis darwinii* 'Nana' and rock garden daphnes.
ZONES 4–9

Clematis fruticosa 'Mongolian Gold'

deciduous shrub

You read that right. This clematis is a selection of a woody, shrubby clematis native to the steppes of China and Mongolia. What does that mean in a garden? This plant blooms in high summer, needs ample drainage to be fully cold-hardy, and is partial to high pH soils. The best plants of it I've seen were in the Denver Botanic Gardens' steppe garden, and southwest of Denver at Kendrick Lake Park. The flowers are butter to bright yellow, and the outside is shiny. It forms a lax shrub easily placed in dryland garden situations, especially grown up-slope or in raised beds, where the red anthers within the cheerful bells are visible.

HEIGHT 2–4 feet (0.5–1.2 m) and as wide
LIGHT EXPOSURE Best with sun from the ground up, all day.
PRUNING Prune any obvious winter dieback once the plant starts to leaf out in early spring. Otherwise, no pruning necessary.
BLOOM TIME July through late September, continuous without deadheading.
LANDSCAPE USE Place in gravel gardens and lime regularly in areas tending to acidic soil. No one who is new to this plant will believe it is a clematis. Great interplanted with blue or violet penstemons, or amongst the shorter forms of *Clematis integrifolia* (as it is at Kendrick Lake Park).
ZONES 4–9

Clematis fusca ◄
herbaceous vine

Ever heard the expression "cute as the fuzz on a bug's ear"? Well, no matter. A bug would search a long time to find cuter fuzz than that on *Clematis fusca*. Or perhaps this is simply a clematis only a collector would love. The flowers are roughly 1 inch (2.5 cm) square, brown with creamy margins, and covered with fuzz—far more hirsute than *C. hirsutissima*, at least on the flowers. In the Viorna Group, this and *C. ianthina* (similar to *C. fusca*, but purple) are the only vining species native outside the New World. At the Rogerson Clematis Garden, *C. fusca* is planted in a woodland garden with other Japanese species. It hails from Japan, China, Korea, Mongolia, and eastern Russia.

HEIGHT 6–7 feet (1.8–2 m)
LIGHT EXPOSURE Partial shade, but does tolerate afternoon sun if sufficiently watered.
PRUNING Hard prune in the winter or early spring. There is little rejuvenation of the upper vines, and it is better to let the whole thing start over every year.
BLOOM TIME Mid-June through late September, continuous with deadheading.
LANDSCAPE USE Place this species where people can see it and be surprised. The little bells aren't showy, but they *are* a conversation starter.
ZONES 3–9

Clematis glaucophylla ▲
herbaceous vine

If clematarians weren't so wild for *Clematis texensis*, I believe this would be the all-time favorite American species. The tailored urn-shaped flowers are deep pink, nearing the shades of some paler *C. texensis* plants. In shady locations with water, *C. glaucophylla* may be almost claret-colored. The margins are creamy to pale yellow, and variation can be seen in a single population. This species was visited in the wilds of Georgia (inside the Chickamauga Battlefield site) by the International Clematis Society in June 2014. The population was in partial "high" shade. It has rotund blue-green leaves. Many of the plants were in a low spot, and others in a riparian zone, along a creek. This species ought to be used in breeding; it is easier to grow than *C. texensis* and likely its progeny would be, too. Prefers soil with a slightly alkaline pH.

HEIGHT 10–16.5 feet (3–5 m)
LIGHT EXPOSURE Partial shade, but does tolerate afternoon sun if sufficiently watered.
PRUNING Hard prune in the winter or early spring. There is little rejuvenation of the upper vines, and it is better to let the whole thing start over every year.
BLOOM TIME Mid-June through mid-September, continuous with deadheading. The seedheads are balls of golden fluff.
LANDSCAPE USE In nature, this winsome species grows in moist soil, wandering through medium-sized deciduous shrubs. Often found with *Rosa palustris* (swamp rose). If it works for mother nature, it should work for us. Hummingbirds love this and are its natural pollinator.
ZONES 6–11

Clematis 'Golden Harvest'

Tangutica/Orientalis Group, deciduous vine

This cultivar is loaded with light golden, dark-centered flowers throughout the summer, followed by wispy silver-tailed seedheads. The flowers are not as big and bold as 'Bill MacKenzie', but they do open out flat, expressing a definite joie de vivre. Named by Chris Sanders, who has made a study of straightening out the muddle in the Tangutica/Orientalis Group. Prolific and vigorous.

HEIGHT 10–13 feet (3–4 m)
LIGHT EXPOSURE Mid- to full sun; especially fine in hot afternoon sun. With enough water, it will tolerate sun from the ground up.
PRUNING Hard prune to 1 foot (30 cm) in late winter.
BLOOM TIME After hard pruning in winter, flowers begin in late June and continue without much encouragement. If flowering flags in hot weather, water more frequently and give a taste of fertilizer.
LANDSCAPE USE This vine makes a superior column on a post that has been wrapped with fencing cloth. Also suitable for creating seasonal shade on an arbor or gazebo, and partners well with the biggest rambling and shrub roses. It can also be grown to great effect in conifers that will tolerate a bit of summer companionship.
ZONES 4–9

Clematis 'Gravetye Beauty'

Texensis Group, herbaceous vine

Yes, this clematis was indeed named for William Robinson's famous English garden, but that is not where it was bred. This is the product of brilliant French hybridizer Francisque Morel, who worked with exceptional forms of *Clematis texensis* as his seed parent to produce some of the most remarkable red clematis ever created. In the present case, the slender blossoms, shaped like lily-flowered tulips, open flat to reveal a luscious red interior. They are nearly as red on the outside as the inside.

HEIGHT 6.5–13 feet (2–4 m)
LIGHT EXPOSURE Best with sun from the ground up, all day.
PRUNING Hard prune in the winter or early spring. There is little rejuvenation of the upper vines, and it is better to let the whole thing start over every year.
BLOOM TIME Mid-June through late September, continuous without deadheading.
LANDSCAPE USE Great with large climbing, rambling, or shrub roses where you want to cover the lower legs with something pretty. Lovely riding roughshod through Japanese bloodgrass (*Imperata cylindrica* 'Rubra'). Makes a good full-sun groundcover.
ZONES 4–9

Clematis 'Helios'

Tangutica/Orientalis Group, deciduous vine

The foliage and poise of this flower suggest more *Clematis orientalis* influence than can be explained by the stated parentage of 'Golden Harvest' × *tangutica*. Be absolutely certain to buy 'Helios' from reputable sources who have propagated it from the true Dutch stock, and who have not grown it from seed. Seedlings of 'Helios' are not 'Helios'. The flowers fling open their bright yellow sepals with gay abandon, and the centers are usually dark, but this can be variable, especially on young plants. The true form of 'Helios' is shorter than its near cousins. If you have a huge 'Helios', it may not be the true form. Along with 'Anita', this is one of the earliest in this group to flower.

HEIGHT 4–6.5 feet (1.2–2 m)
LIGHT EXPOSURE Mid- to full sun; especially fine in hot afternoon sun. It will tolerate sun from the ground up.
PRUNING Hard prune to 1 foot (30 cm) in late winter.
BLOOM TIME After hard pruning in winter, flowers begin in June, and continue without much encouragement. If flowering falls off a bit in hot weather, water more frequently and give a taste of fertilizer.
LANDSCAPE USE This vine makes a superior column on a post that has been wrapped with fencing cloth. Also effective when allowed to ramble through sturdy ornamental grasses, such as *Panicum virgatum* 'Heavy Metal', *Miscanthus sinensis* 'Gold Bar', and *M. s.* 'Gold Breeze'.
ZONES 4–9

Clematis 'Helsingborg'

Atragene Group, deciduous vine

A couple of species in the Atragene Group are capable of bestowing a pale outline to the rich color of their hybrids. In this case, *Clematis ochotensis* gives the lighter margin to the rich purple of 'Helsingborg'. This is thought by some to have the most saturated purple in this group, and perhaps the pale outline of the sepals emphasizes the depth of hue.

HEIGHT 6.5–13 feet (2–4 m)
LIGHT EXPOSURE Mid- to full sun. Shaded roots preferred, and gravel rather than organic mulch.
PRUNING Prune as needed after the first wave of blooms is spent, giving the vine the remainder of the growing season to recover. In areas with very cold winters, do not remove the old leaves as they curl around the nodes. This is probably an adaptation to the cold, protecting the latent buds in the node for the coming year.
BLOOM TIME Mid-April through mid-May with good rebloom in 60–90 days.
LANDSCAPE USE Excellent on a flat-panel trellis or fences, in white lilacs and over rhododendrons, decorating evergreen hedges.
ZONES 4–9

Clematis heracleifolia 'Cassandra'

Heracleifolia Group, deciduous subshrub

The Heracleifolia Group is composed of generally similar plants, all woody sub-shrubs with blue flowers that bloom in July and August. The strong flower stems rise well above the coarse green foliage. Rather than mention many, I will limit myself to the best, 'Cassandra'. Simply put, it has the best color (nearly cobalt blue), the largest florets, and the best scent. In fact, I'd go so far as to say it is my favorite scent of *any* fragrant clematis. To me, it is the comforting fragrance of suntan lotion. Like any of this group, which includes hybrids involving *Clematis tubulosa*, it is drought tolerant once established.

HEIGHT 3–3.5 feet (0.75–1 m)
LIGHT EXPOSURE Full sun.
PRUNING Hard prune in the winter or early spring. There is little rejuvenation of the upper wood, so take off all non-rejuvenating wood in late March.
BLOOM TIME July through August, longer with deadheading.
LANDSCAPE USE Great amongst the late daylilies, heleniums, coreopsis, and early Michaelmas daisies. Use when you want a blue-flowering plant to complete a primary color trio in the high summer garden.
ZONES 5–9

Clematis hirsutissima

herbaceous perennial

The entirety of this diminutive species (commonly known as sugar bowls) is covered with fine white hairs, including the purple-blue flowers. Other color forms, such as cotton-candy pink, have been found in its native range, the high elevations of the western United States, especially in the Rocky Mountains. The foliage is highly dissected, even thread-like in some populations, and appears silver-gray when grown in full sun. Maximum light produces the most hair. Greenhouse-grown specimens may not appear to be particularly hirsute.

HEIGHT 12–30 inches (30–75 cm) and as broad, when mature

LIGHT EXPOSURE Full sun.

PRUNING Dies down to nothing during winter dormancy; simply clean up the old carcass.

BLOOM TIME Depends upon how quickly the soil warms, May through mid-July. I have seen this in full bloom in early October at the Denver Botanic Gardens; because the seed was harvested for propagation, the plant rebloomed into the autumn.

LANDSCAPE USE If you are gardening outside the plant's native range, climate, and soil conditions (high pH), grow in full-sun gravel gardens or troughs. Needs to be positioned where the soil warms quickly in the spring, or it will not bloom.

ZONES 3–8

Clematis '*Huldine*' ❀

Viticella Group, deciduous vine

Again we are given a clematis claiming to be a late large-flowered hybrid that carries all the hallmarks of the Viticella Group, so I include it there. The flowers are smaller, the vine more vigorous, and I have not seen this plant produce spring flowers (which a true late large-flowered hybrid would do if left unpruned). 'Huldine' flowers strictly on new growth and needs a great deal of hot sun to do so. The creamy blossoms have sepals both deeply grooved and "hipped"; the sepal points dip down. The reverses are barred with mauve-purple veins, giving the creamy color a silvery cast.

HEIGHT 9–20 feet (2.5–6 m)

LIGHT EXPOSURE Mid- to full sun; must have nearly full sun to flower well. Especially fine in hot afternoon sun. It will tolerate sun from the ground up.

PRUNING Hard prune to 1 foot (30 cm) in late winter.

BLOOM TIME After hard pruning in winter, flowers in July/August. This plant responds well to manipulation of standard pruning advice. If pruned by one-half its length after the first wave of bloom, it will rebloom from autumn to frost in temperate climates.

LANDSCAPE USE Gorgeous combined with late-flowering rambling roses and vigorous modern climbers such as 'New Dawn'. This clematis is especially complementary to other flowers with silver-lavender flowers.

ZONES 4–9

Clematis Inspiration 'Zoin'

Integrifolia Group, herbaceous perennial

This pink-flowered hybrid has a depth of color we can best attribute to its near-red large-flowered parent, 'Warszawska Nike' Midnight Showers. Again we see that a vigorous climber, when crossed with a selection of *Clematis integrifolia*—in this case 'Rosea'—does not produce a climber. I first saw this many years ago in the garden of Jane Gay in Vancouver, B.C., wandering through a lavender mophead hydrangea. It was a charming effect.

HEIGHT 5–6.5 feet (1.5–2 m).
LIGHT EXPOSURE Full sun, six hours a day or more.
PRUNING Since this is an herbaceous perennial, hard pruning down to a few inches tall after dormancy in late autumn or winter is a necessity. All new growth comes from the base.
BLOOM TIME May and June. Cut back by half its length after flowering (or hard prune again) to spur a second flowering in late summer, usually from late August into the autumn.
LANDSCAPE USE A worthy partner for medium to large shrub roses and hydrangeas of any sort that will tolerate plenty of sun if sufficiently watered.
ZONES 4–9

Clematis integrifolia ❀

herbaceous perennial

Native throughout northern Europe east to the chilly shores of Lake Baikal, this may be the hardiest of the hardy perennial clematis. It is also one of the earliest species used in breeding, in the 1830s. Usually around 2 feet (0.5 m) tall, finding a dwarf form in the wild has long been a Holy Grail. The type flower is purplish blue, with four sepals in a nodding bell. The sepals may also twist like a corkscrew, or flip open like birds' wings. White, shades of blue, and pink variants have been found and named. The foliage has no petioles (botanically, the leaves are sessile) and cannot climb. This trait is highly dominant when *Clematis integrifolia* is used in crosses. It is scented; the white variants are more so.

HEIGHT 2 feet (0.5 m).
LIGHT EXPOSURE Full sun for maximum flowering.
PRUNING Hard prune in the winter or early spring. New growth comes entirely from underground shoots or basal buds at soil level.
BLOOM TIME Late May through late September, continuous with deadheading.
LANDSCAPE USE Well suited for any mixed perennial border. The early growth may flop, and a peony cage placed surrounding the crown when new shoots appear will prevent this. Plants hard pruned in midsummer (around Bastille Day) will be sturdier and flower until frost.
ZONES 3–9

Clematis integrifolia 'Alba'

Integrifolia Group, herbaceous perennial

It is most accurately said that 'Alba' is a selection of *Clematis integrifolia*, which shows an interesting variation of colors in the wild. Seeds of a white form obtained through a Canadian source were sent to Magnus Johnson in Sweden, and he grew them out to select the best seedling. Growing 'Alba' from seed rarely produces a pure white flower. At its best the nodding white flowers are fragrant (the most fragrant of this group) and of good substance, with yellow to white stamens. Seedlings may have a blue cast or blue midrib but more likely will look like *C. integrifolia* in every way. There is no discernible difference between this and Gazelle 'Evipo014'.

HEIGHT 4 feet (1.2 m) or less
LIGHT EXPOSURE Full sun, six hours a day or more.
PRUNING Since this is an herbaceous perennial, hard pruning down to a few inches tall after dormancy in late autumn or winter is a necessity. All new growth comes from the base.
BLOOM TIME May and June. Cut back by half its length after flowering (or hard prune again) to spur a second flowering in late summer, usually from late August into the autumn.
LANDSCAPE USE Well able to decorate the lower branches of spring- or summer-flowering shrubs. Alternatively, grow in a peony cage, as a specimen herbaceous perennial, to get the flowers more closely up to nose level.
ZONES 2–9

Clematis integrifolia Mongolian Bells 'PSHarlan'

Integrifolia Group, herbaceous perennial

Harlan Hamernik collected seed of *Clematis integrifolia* from a mixed-color population in Mongolia. Plants of blue, lavender-pink, or white flowers were subsequently introduced to the US trade, as the seed strain Mongolian Bells, through the Plant Select program in the Rocky Mountain region. Denver Botanic Gardens hosts trials and suggests plants for Plant Select.

HEIGHT less than 36 inches (1 m)
LIGHT EXPOSURE Full sun, six hours a day or more.
PRUNING Since this is an herbaceous perennial, hard pruning down to a few inches tall after dormancy in late autumn or winter is a necessity. All new growth comes from the base.
BLOOM TIME May and June. Deadhead after flowering (or hard prune again) to spur a second flowering in late summer, usually from late August into the autumn.
LANDSCAPE USE The compact habit of this seed strain means the plants are mound-formers rather than ramblers. Great in gravel gardens and hellstrips—anywhere a free-flowering, drought-tolerant herbaceous perennial is needed for a drought-stressed site.
ZONES 3–9

Clematis japonica
deciduous vine

This seductive woodland native has been in cultivation in the West since the 1780s. The smooth 1-inch (2.5-cm) bells are mahogany or rosy brown, often creamy where the sepals attach to their peduncle (at a structure known as the receptacle). It is a subtle flower, meant to be seen up close. *Clematis japonica* var. *obvallata* differs in having two little bracteoles right above the blossoms, adding to the charm (some experts grant this enhanced flower specific status). A couple of variegated forms are also occasionally seen in the trade.

HEIGHT 7–9 feet (2–3 m)
LIGHT EXPOSURE Partial shade, but does tolerate afternoon sun if sufficiently watered.
PRUNING Remove only what may have died back during the winter, as this flowers on the previous year's growth. If it outgrows its space or threatens a living host, hard prune to 3 feet (1 m) immediately after flowering and fertilize.
BLOOM TIME May and June.
LANDSCAPE USE Very effective in woodlands. Protect from afternoon sun. In the Pacific Northwest it partners well with vine maple (*Acer circinatum*).
ZONES 6–10

Clematis 'Jenny'
Montana Group, deciduous vine

Breeder Alister Keay named this plant for his petite wife, Jenny, and wished the plant to be known as 'Jenny Keay', but when he first mentioned it in writing, he called it 'Jenny', so that is the official cultivar name. You will often find it with the full name. This selection is indeed as elfin as its namesake, at least by *Clematis montana* standards. The long-lasting flowers are small and very double, creamy on the shady side of the vine and more pink in full sun. This may be the only clematis in the Montana Group suitable for small gardens or large containers.

HEIGHT to 16.5 feet (5 m)
LIGHT EXPOSURE Mid- to full sun. Tolerates partial shade better than any other in the Montana Group.
PRUNING Prune to whatever degree necessary in late June, after flowering. This gives the plant the growing season to recover enough to flower on time the next year. Many in the Montana Group benefit from a rejuvenating hard pruning every 3–5 years.
BLOOM TIME Late April to mid-June.
LANDSCAPE USE Rarely getting bigger than about 15 feet (4.5 m), this vine shows a marked tendency to creep along, making it ideal as a thick groundcover. If you want it to grow up, use a built structure of sufficient strength, or a tree already mature.
ZONES 7–10

Clematis John Howells 'Zojohnhowells'

Viticella Group, deciduous vine

The name of this Dutch cultivar honors John Howells, the Viticella Group's great champion. We don't know the parentage of this memorial clematis, but the flowers are plumper than is typical for the group, so one wonders if a particularly fine large-flowered hybrid, perhaps one of the brilliant red Polish cultivars, or an old classic like 'Rouge Cardinal' or 'Crimson King' wasn't back-bred into the lineage to make a greater red statement. In any case, the color is vibrant.

HEIGHT 9–12 feet (3–3.5 m)
LIGHT EXPOSURE Mid- to full sun; especially fine in hot afternoon sun. Shaded roots preferred, but with enough water, it will tolerate sun from the ground up.
PRUNING Hard prune to 1 foot (30 cm) in late winter.
BLOOM TIME After hard pruning in winter, flowers in July/August. This plant responds well to manipulation of standard pruning advice. If pruned by one-half its length after the first wave of bloom, it will rebloom from autumn to frost in temperate climates.
LANDSCAPE USE This gives a fabulous effect combined with gray-foliaged plants such as *Pyrus salicifolia* 'Pendula' (silver weeping pear). Also effective wandering spangled amongst the frothy variegation of *Salix integra* 'Hakuro-nishiki', with its splashes of pink.
ZONES 5–9

Clematis 'Juuli' ❀

Integrifolia Group, herbaceous perennial

Juuli means "July" in Estonian, and in Estonia, that's when 'Juuli' produces its lavender to sky blue flowers. This is similar to 'Arabella' but can get taller, and the flowers slightly larger. In more temperate long-season climates, flowering starts earlier, often early June.

HEIGHT 3.5–5 feet (1–1.5 m)
LIGHT EXPOSURE Full sun, six hours a day or more.
PRUNING Since this is an herbaceous perennial, hard pruning down to a few inches tall after dormancy in late autumn or winter is a necessity. All new growth comes from the base.
BLOOM TIME May and June. Cut back by half its length after flowering (or hard prune again) to spur a second flowering in late summer, usually from late August into the autumn.
LANDSCAPE USE Makes a wonderful groundcover if crowns are planted on 36-inch (1-m) centers. This flower is a lovely contrasting color for yellow and peach shrub roses.
ZONES 3–9

Clematis koreana var. fragrans

Atragene Group, deciduous vine

This naturally occurring variety of *Clematis koreana* was brought into the trade from a plant collecting expedition mounted by Norway's Nordic Arboretum. What is available now is often grown from seed, and the amount of fragrance can vary widely. The color is mahogany (red-brown) to pale rose, and most blossoms will show spurs on the sepals where they curve into the receptacle. Very free-flowering. Any fragrance is most noticeable during warm mornings or evenings. There is also a fine, wine-colored outline on the leaflets, especially early in the season.

HEIGHT 9–12 feet (3–3.5 m)

LIGHT EXPOSURE Mid- to full sun. Shaded roots preferred, and gravel rather than organic mulch.

PRUNING Prune as needed after the first wave of blooms is spent, giving the vine the remainder of the growing season to recover. In areas with very cold winters, do not remove the old leaves as they curl around the nodes. This is probably an adaptation to the cold, protecting the latent buds in the node for the coming year.

BLOOM TIME Mid-April through mid-May and beyond. The color will be pale in hot weather, and nearly as dark as 'Brunette' when nights are cold during bud set.

LANDSCAPE USE The best use of this plant I've seen is letting it ramble through *Deutzia setchuenensis* var. *corymbiflora*, which has corymbs (as luck would have it) of starry white florets throughout much of the spring and summer.

ZONES 3–8

Clematis 'Lord Herschell'

Integrifolia Group, herbaceous perennial

This is the nearest red yet produced of any cultivar in the Integrifolia Group. One might wish it was quicker to make a bulky plant, and that the flowers were more freely produced, but it is a lovely thing. Given that the same breeder, Barry Fretwell, used a large-flowered hybrid to create *Clematis ×diversifolia* 'Heather Herschell', and that Fretwell has named multiple siblings from other crosses (witness 'Arabella' and 'Miranda'), we might assume "Heather" and "his lordship" are siblings, or at least that a very fine red large-flowered hybrid is in the genetics here somewhere.

HEIGHT 3 feet (1 m) or less
LIGHT EXPOSURE Full sun, six hours a day or more.
PRUNING Since this is an herbaceous perennial, hard pruning down to a few inches tall after dormancy in late autumn or winter is a necessity. All new growth comes from the base.
BLOOM TIME May and June. Cut back by half its length after flowering (or hard prune again) to spur a second flowering in late summer, usually from late August into the autumn.
LANDSCAPE USE Well able to decorate the lower branches of spring- or summer-flowering shrubs, or grow in a peony cage to present as a specimen herbaceous perennial.
ZONES 2–9

Clematis 'Lunar Lass'

Evergreen Group, semi-evergreen/evergreen non-clinging vine

This is yet another instance of the smallest known clematis crossed with another New Zealand countryman, *Clematis marata*. The result is a lacy-foliaged non-climber of greater winter hardiness than is generally assumed. The key to success is ample drainage. The buds and flowers are initially pistachio green—the moon is made of green cheese, remember, hence the name—but mature to cream. The lax slender stems are weighed down by the volume of bloom.

HEIGHT to 3.5 feet (1 m)
LIGHT EXPOSURE Partial shade to full sun.
PRUNING Prune to whatever degree necessary in May after flowering. This gives the plant a growing season to recover enough to flower on time the next year. Generally evergreen, but occasionally there may be some dieback of old stems after flowering. Just remove the old growth to the soil surface, carefully avoiding damage to any emergent new growth.
BLOOM TIME April into May.
LANDSCAPE USE Lovely in standing containers so the drape of the stems can be appreciated. Also ideal in a gravel garden as a groundcover.
ZONES 7–9

Clematis 'Madame Julia Correvon'
Viticella Group, deciduous vine

As you might have heard by now, red in clematis is a relative term. One important variable is night temperature as the flower buds are forming. In hot weather, allegedly red clematis will be nearer to true red. Consistently reddest of all is 'Madame Julia Correvon'. The other wonderful thing about this plant is the pose of the flowers—gappy, twisty, distinctive. No other red clematis is like it. Even on a still day, there is a motion, an enthusiasm, to this vine that is beguiling. This is one of the oldest *Clematis viticella* hybrids to boast *C. texensis* as a grandparent, hence the solid intensity of the red. 'Rubra Grandiflora' × 'Ville de Lyon'. Flower diameter 4 inches (10 cm).

HEIGHT 9–12 feet (3–3.5 m)

LIGHT EXPOSURE Mid- to full sun; especially fine in hot afternoon sun. Shaded roots preferred, but with enough water, it will tolerate sun from the ground up.

PRUNING Hard prune to 1 foot (30 cm) in late winter.

BLOOM TIME After hard pruning in winter, flowers in July/August. This plant responds well to manipulation of standard pruning advice. If pruned by one-half its length after the first wave of bloom, it will rebloom from autumn to frost in temperate climates.

LANDSCAPE USE This vine makes a superior column on a post that has been wrapped with fencing cloth. Without a vertical nearby, it will romp over groundcovers, as seen in Beth Chatto's garden running through *Epimedium pinnatum* subsp. *colchicum*. If planted 4–6 feet (1.2–1.8 m) from other vines to avoid root competition, it makes an outstanding companion. In Pam Frost's garden in Vancouver, B.C., this grows into golden hop (*Humulus lupulus* 'Aureus') to great effect.

ZONES 3–11

Clematis mandshurica

herbaceous perennial

Imagine a lax-climbing version of *Clematis flammula*, and you have its close cousin, *C. mandshurica* (reduced by "lumpers" to a variety of *C. terniflora*). The plant does not begin to climb until the overall height reaches 3 feet (1 m) or so, and even then, the grasp is tenuous. The fluffy white inflorescence is made up of small four-sepalled blossoms. The flowering stems are widely used in Japan as a gypsophila-like filler in flower arrangements, but this has a much finer fragrance.

HEIGHT 3.5–7 feet (1.5–2 m)
LIGHT EXPOSURE Full sun.
PRUNING Hard prune in the winter or early spring; treat as an herbaceous perennial.
BLOOM TIME Late June through September.
LANDSCAPE USE Great for the cutting garden, or use as a frothy filler throughout the garden. The autumn color of the seeds is wonderful.
ZONES 4–9

Clematis 'Markham's Pink' ✻

Atragene Group, deciduous vine

For a nice cotton-candy pink ballet skirt, this cultivar has been equaled but never bettered. The reverses (outside surface) of the four sepals are darker than the interior, giving the color more drama from a distance than you'd expect from a pink blossom. The shading is more vivid as the first buds form during cool nights, and the August rebloom stands up well to the sun.

HEIGHT 6–7 feet (1.8–2 m)
LIGHT EXPOSURE Mid- to full sun. Shaded roots preferred, and gravel rather than organic mulch.

PRUNING Prune as needed after the first wave of blooms is spent, giving the vine the remainder of the growing season to recover. In areas with very cold winters, do not remove the old leaves as they curl around the nodes. This is probably an adaptation to the cold, protecting the latent buds in the node for the coming year.

BLOOM TIME Mid-April through mid-May with good rebloom in 60–90 days.
LANDSCAPE USE Makes a nice background, grown on a flat-panel trellis.
ZONES 3–8

Clematis 'Minuet' ❖

Viticella Group, deciduous vine

This fine and long-lived vine is one of a suite of hybrids bred by Francisque Morel, and sent along to William Robinson of Gravetye Manor when Morel closed up shop in about 1900. Most of the cultivars were subsequently named by Robinson's head gardener, Ernest Markham, and introduced to the trade in Great Britain. 'Minuet' is a charming smaller version of 'Venosa Violacea' (1883), with the typical pagoda roof rather than being upfacing and flat. The flowers are fundamentally white with purple/cerise veining (the color seems weather dependent), which forms an outline of purple-to-cerise at the margins.

HEIGHT 7–10 feet (2–3 m)

LIGHT EXPOSURE Mid- to full sun; especially fine in hot afternoon sun. Shaded roots preferred, but with enough water, it will tolerate sun from the ground up.

PRUNING Hard prune to 1 foot (30 cm) in late winter.

BLOOM TIME After hard pruning in winter, flowers in July/August. This plant responds well to manipulation of standard pruning advice. If pruned by one-half its length after the first wave of bloom, it will rebloom from autumn to frost in temperate climates.

LANDSCAPE USE 'Minuet' is charming as the anchor of a display of other vines, especially *Rhodochiton atrosanguineus* (purplebell vine), and annual climbers such as morning glories (*Ipomoea*).

ZONES 3–11

Clematis 'Miranda'

Integrifolia Group, herbaceous perennial

This cultivar is the less-well-known sister of the widely popular 'Arabella'. Since I like dramatic colors, I prefer 'Miranda', with her more saturated dark lavender-blue flowers. Also, in this case the flowers are somewhat larger and the plant lankier. Close examination leads one to wonder if Barry Fretwell wasn't trying to recreate *Clematis* ×*durandii* with a modern *integrifolia* × *lanuginosa* pairing.

HEIGHT 4–7 feet (1.2–2 m) or less
LIGHT EXPOSURE Full sun, six hours a day or more.
PRUNING Since this is an herbaceous perennial, hard pruning down to a few inches tall after dormancy in late autumn or winter is a necessity. All new growth comes from the base.
BLOOM TIME May and June. Cut back by half its length after flowering (or hard prune again) to spur a second flowering in late summer, usually from late August into the autumn.
LANDSCAPE USE Well able to decorate the lower branches of spring- or summer-flowering shrubs, tall bearded iris, and roses.
ZONES 5–8

Clematis montana var. *wilsonii* hort.

Montana Group, deciduous vine

When you see the notation "hort." after a plant name, rest assured some confusion is sure to follow. That designation indicates the plant available in the horticulture trade is using a name that may not be its own or that is applied accidentally to more than one plant. The plant E. H. Wilson collected in China and initially described in his notes and herbarium specimens is much different from what we now grow as var. *wilsonii*. John Howells suggested this selection be called 'White Fragrance', but the moniker never caught on, descriptive though it is. This clematis is indeed creamy white and is strongly scented of chocolate. It flowers only slightly later than the main wave of Montana Group cultivars.

HEIGHT 23 feet (7 m) or more
LIGHT EXPOSURE Mid- to full sun. Although a poor choice for complete shade, this vine flowers equally well if half in deciduous shade and half facing south.
PRUNING Prune to whatever degree necessary in late June, after flowering. This gives the plant the growing season to recover enough to flower on time the next year. Many in the Montana Group benefit from a rejuvenating hard pruning every 3–5 years. You can take a hedge trimmer to this vine in late June, and by late August it will have restored itself.
BLOOM TIME Mid-May to late June, with some modest random rebloom.
LANDSCAPE USE Use this to cover a long cyclone fence, a large shed, or small mansion, or allow it to roam over a large rock wall.
ZONES 7–10

Clematis 'Mrs. Robert Brydon'

Heracleifolia Group, semi-herbaceous
subshrub

This is a big, floppy girl, but the ice blue flowers and large trifoliate leaves make this a great cover-up for areas planted with bulbs. As the tulips or narcissus fade into dormancy, 'Mrs. Robert Brydon' will discreetly cover their remains. If you want to use this as a flowering large-leafed screen plant, it will need to be tied into place.

HEIGHT 6–7 feet (1.8–2 m)
LIGHT EXPOSURE Full sun.

PRUNING Hard prune in the winter or early spring, leaving lower woody growth showing newly emerging buds.
BLOOM TIME Mid-June through late September, continuous with deadheading.
LANDSCAPE USE Use over embankments, and as a groundcover to hide out-of-bloom bulb foliage. Blooms at the same time as frikartii asters, making a wonderful August showing.
ZONES 5–9

Clematis 'Odoriba'

Texensis Group, herbaceous vine

Despite its often being grouped with hybrids involving *Clematis texensis*, there is no hint of *C. texensis* in the breeding (verified as *viorna* × *crispa*) of this versatile clematis. The often rosy red exterior and bloom shape might cause us to infer a relationship that does not exist. The hint to the truth is the existence of a white bar on the interior of the sepals, telltale proof that *C. crispa* had a hand in the begetting of this cultivar. This vine was originally bred for the Japanese cut flower market. Tolerant of excessively moist soil conditions.

HEIGHT 7–9 feet (2–3 m)

LIGHT EXPOSURE Partial shade to full sun.

PRUNING Hard prune in the winter or early spring. There is little rejuvenation of the upper vines, and it is better to let the whole thing start over every year.

BLOOM TIME Late June through late September, continuous without deadheading.

LANDSCAPE USE Produces a lovely display on a flat-panel trellis on its own or growing into small trees. Not overly heavy, so not a thuggish partner. Appealing with *Fuchsia* 'Whiteknights Amethyst' and other large hardy fuchsias.

ZONES 5–10

Clematis otophora

semi-evergreen vine

Two slightly varying forms of this brilliant shade-loving vine are circulating in the trade, with the only difference being that the form from Far Reaches Farm in Port Townsend, Washington, from their own collection in China, has a longer, slightly more elegant bell than the boxier form available seed-grown in Europe. Both versions come rapidly from cuttings or seed. Think of this as a high-climbing 'Bells of Emei Shan', with the bright yellow bells on long peduncles.

HEIGHT 6–7 feet (1.8–2 m)
LIGHT EXPOSURE Partial shade, but does tolerate afternoon sun if sufficiently watered.
PRUNING In early spring prune only what has obviously died back during the winter. If the vines become too rampant, cut back by half in mid- to late May when the plant is in active growth. This will delay the bloom time.
BLOOM TIME July through autumn, continuous without deadheading.
LANDSCAPE USE The bright yellow color really shines amongst dark conifers such as *Cryptomeria japonica* 'Black Dragon'. Great on a structure as a solo act, or draping over a stumpery with 'Bells of Emei Shan' creeping along the ground at its feet, perhaps with some blue hosta.
ZONES 6–10 (seen blooming beautifully in Spokane, Washington, where the gardener assured me the garden was at a zone 5 elevation)

Clematis 'Pamiat Serdsta'

Integrifolia Group, herbaceous perennial

The name, translated from Ukrainian, is "memory from the heart." This member of the Integrifolia Group has *Clematis lanuginosa* in its background, too, via the white cultivar 'Candida'. For many years I fretted that this and 'Alionushka' were one and the same, but as it turned out, I was being sold 'Alionushka' over and over. Queen of the Misnamed Plants, that's me. When I finally latched onto the right thing, the differences became obvious. 'Pamiat Serdsta' is a striking deep violet, with widely flaring sepals. This also gets much taller than 'Alionushka'.

HEIGHT 5–7 feet (1.5–2 m)
LIGHT EXPOSURE Full sun, six hours a day or more.
PRUNING Since this is an herbaceous perennial, hard pruning down to a few inches tall after dormancy in late autumn or winter is a necessity. All new growth comes from the base.
BLOOM TIME May and June. Cut back by half its length after flowering (or hard prune again) to spur a second flowering in late summer, usually from late August into the autumn.
LANDSCAPE USE Lovely with white, peach, and yellow shrub roses, and tall late-season yellow to gold herbaceous perennial plants. Also makes a fine groundcover.
ZONES 3–9

Clematis 'Pangbourne Pink'

Integrifolia Group, herbaceous perennial

Of the many good examples of pink *Clematis integrifolia* hybrids, this might be my favorite. It makes a full bushy mound, covered with mid-pink flowers over a long period. It is hard to argue with success and exuberance.

HEIGHT 3 feet (1 m) or less
LIGHT EXPOSURE Full sun, six hours a day or more.

PRUNING Since this is an herbaceous perennial, hard pruning down to a few inches tall after dormancy in late autumn or winter is a necessity. All new growth comes from the base.
BLOOM TIME May and June, then deadhead to continue in late July through autumn.
LANDSCAPE USE Nice as a mounding specimen in a mixed perennial border.
ZONES 4–9

Clematis Petit Faucon 'Evisix'

Integrifolia Group, herbaceous perennial

The name (French for "little falcon") is aptly descriptive of the shape of the sepals, which dip and twist like falcon wings. The seed parent was large-flowered hybrid 'Daniel Deronda', which explains the beauty of the color. This also has a dark eye with light anthers, like it's winking at you. Perhaps this should have been "Saucy Falcon"?

HEIGHT 3.5–5 feet (1–1.5 m)
LIGHT EXPOSURE Full sun, six hours a day or more.

PRUNING Since this is an herbaceous perennial, hard pruning down to a few inches tall after dormancy in late autumn or winter is a necessity. All new growth comes from the base.
BLOOM TIME May and June. Cut back by half its length after flowering (or hard prune again) to spur a second flowering in late summer, usually from late August into the autumn.
LANDSCAPE USE The early flowers are lovely with mock-orange (*Philadelphus*), especially *P.* 'Belle Étoile'. Then Petit Faucon will continue to decorate the shrub when it's gone out of bloom.
ZONES 4–9

Clematis pitcheri
herbaceous vine

This vine is often mistaken for other species but in fact has distinct flowers you won't forget once you've seen the real thing. It cross pollinates promiscuously with other species in the Viorna Group, and for this reason inferior hybrids arise rather constantly from seed exchanges. The flowers should be shiny silver-lavender on the outside; this is especially noticeable in full sun. The interior of the sepals, where the tips flare out, is plush dark purple, often nearly black. Anything else is a hybrid, and if the seed has come from odd geographically isolated populations (such as those in Texas), it may represent a newly documented species accidentally lumped into *Clematis pitcheri* when first recorded.

HEIGHT 6–7 feet (1.8–2 m)
LIGHT EXPOSURE Partial shade, but does tolerate more sun if sufficiently watered.
PRUNING Hard prune in the winter or early spring. There is little rejuvenation of the upper vines, and it is better to let the whole thing start over every year.
BLOOM TIME Mid-June through late September, continuous without deadheading.
LANDSCAPE USE Give this vine a light background to show off the fascinating little urns. Great amongst white or yellow roses, and can be pruned whenever the roses are pruned in the winter because the previous year's growth will not rejuvenate.
ZONES 4–9

Clematis '*Polish Spirit*' ❋

Viticella Group, deciduous vine

This is a great clematis in every way. It boasts a lovely, carrying shade of violet-purple, not so dark as to disappear from a distance. The color blends well with any of the yellow small-flowered hybrids, and the texture is sufficiently interesting to pair well with large-flowered hybrids, too. If you want a clematis to bloom all summer, this is as close as you'll come.

HEIGHT 10–13 feet (3–4 m)

LIGHT EXPOSURE Mid- to full sun; especially fine in hot afternoon sun. Shaded roots preferred, but with enough water, it will tolerate sun from the ground up.

PRUNING Hard prune to 1 foot (30 cm) in late winter.

BLOOM TIME After hard pruning in winter, flowers in July/August. This plant responds well to manipulation of standard pruning advice. If pruned by one-half its length after the first wave of bloom, it will rebloom from autumn to frost in temperate climates.

LANDSCAPE USE Other than producing huge purple flowers or staying short, this clematis will do whatever you ask of it. Flower all summer? Yes, with sufficient water and some light grooming. Mingle without mangling? Yes; although vigorous, the canes are not heavy. Combine well with other colors? Yes; one cannot imagine this pleasing violet-purple clashing with anything.

ZONES 3–9

Clematis 'Prince Charles' ✳

Viticella Group, deciduous vine

Yes, we are quite well aware the person who introduced it as a chance seedling, Alister Keay of New Zealand, lists this cultivar as a late large-flowered hybrid. Given the unknown provenance (it may be a much older lost *lanuginosa* × *viticella* hybrid), the size and texture of the flower, and the growth habit, the vine is much better included in the Viticella Group. Often called "the poor man's 'Perle d'Azur'"—let's hope His Royal Highness has not heard this. 'Prince Charles' has a slightly lighter and more lavender color than the periwinkle blue of 'Perle d'Azur'.

HEIGHT 5–10 feet (1.5–3 m)
LIGHT EXPOSURE Mid- to full sun. Shaded roots preferred, but with enough water, it will tolerate sun from the ground up.
PRUNING Hard prune to 1 foot (30 cm) in late winter.
BLOOM TIME After hard pruning in winter, flowers in July/August. This plant responds well to manipulation of standard pruning advice. If pruned by one-half its length after the first wave of bloom, it will rebloom from autumn to frost in temperate climates.
LANDSCAPE USE Excellent with other clematis with strong shades of pink—'Comtesse de Bouchaud', Alaina 'Evipo056', and . . . dare I suggest a popular pink *Clematis texensis* hybrid, such as 'Duchess of Albany'? Harumph. What did you *think* I was going to suggest?
ZONES 4–10

Clematis 'Princess Diana' ✿

Texensis Group, herbaceous vine

This is in many ways an improved 'Duchess of Albany'. There is less tendency to grow wild without flowering, and the color is a stronger rosy pink. 'Princess Diana' has the typical Texensis Group shape. The size of the vine is more compact, and the volume of flowers is impressive. Introduced in 1984 and already a classic.

HEIGHT 6–7 feet (1.8–2 m)
LIGHT EXPOSURE Best with sun from the ground up, all day.
PRUNING Hard prune in the winter or early spring. There is little rejuvenation of the upper vines, and it is better to let the whole thing start over every year.
BLOOM TIME Mid-June through late September, continuous without deadheading.
LANDSCAPE USE Great with large climbing, rambling, or shrub roses, where you want to cover the lower legs with something pretty. Makes an unusual rock garden or gravel garden groundcover, especially under lilies such as *Lilium sargentiae*, which also need full sun.
ZONES 4–9

Clematis Princess Kate 'Zoprika'

Texensis Group, herbaceous vine

This clematis marks a new color combination in the Texensis Group. The "tulips," similar in shape to 'Princess Diana' but with more substance, are creamy white with a unique rosy violet reverse. Looking into the center of the blossoms, one has the impression of a dark eye, enhanced by purply filaments and purple-red anthers. The flowers may be either out- or upfacing. This would be a great plant no matter who it was named after, but there's nothing like naming something after an attractive young British royal to sell plants.

HEIGHT 6–7 feet (1.8–2 m)
LIGHT EXPOSURE Best with sun from the ground up, all day.
PRUNING Hard prune in the winter or early spring. There is little rejuvenation of the upper vines, and it is better to let the whole thing start over every year.
BLOOM TIME Mid-June through late September, continuous without deadheading.
LANDSCAPE USE This will be a perfect back-of-the-border drapery on a fence or flat-panel trellis. The vines are not heavy, and the options are endless as long as the sun requirement is met.
ZONES 7–9, and probably hardier

Clematis 'Purpurea Plena Elegans'

Viticella Group, deciduous vine

The name notwithstanding, the color of these boisterous little pompons is dusty rose, not purple. Just hold it up next to its much more purple doppelgänger, *Clematis viticella* 'Flore Pleno', and you will see that "PPE," as we call it at home, is much more pink. The flowers can be nearly as thick as they are wide. This cultivar does very well left unpruned for years at a time, wandering through *Cornus florida* and other large cornels, where it will enliven the tree between spring flowering and autumn color and fruit.

HEIGHT 10.5–13 feet (3–4 m)

LIGHT EXPOSURE Mid- to full sun; especially fine in hot afternoon sun. Shaded roots preferred, but with enough water, it will tolerate sun from the ground up.

PRUNING Hard prune to 1 foot (30 cm) in late winter.

BLOOM TIME After hard pruning in winter, flowers in July/August. This plant responds well to manipulation of standard pruning advice. If pruned by one-half its length after the first wave of bloom, it will rebloom from autumn to frost in temperate climates.

LANDSCAPE USE Excellent in small trees or tumbling through large rhododendrons allowed to grow to tree size and limbed-up.

ZONES 4–10

Clematis recta 'Midnight Masquerade'

Flammula Group, herbaceous perennial

Urs Baltensparger of Edelweiss Nursery in Canby, Oregon, has done a lot of selecting within the available *Clematis recta* 'Purpurea' forms, but this is by far the best of his seedlings and, hands down, the darkest-foliaged version of that species variant. The newly emergent foliage stays nearly black-purple until the fragrant white flowers start to bloom in late May/early June. Once flowering has stopped (around Bastille Day), hard prune the plant, and the new growth will stay shorter but will be just as divinely dark.

HEIGHT 3.5–5 feet (1–1.5 m)

LIGHT EXPOSURE Tolerates partial shade, but full sun enhances the color.

PRUNING Hard prune in the winter or early spring. New growth is marred by the old dead foliage from the previous year.

BLOOM TIME Late May through early July, reblooms after second summer hard prune.

LANDSCAPE USE Because the new growth is so thrillingly dark, place with a gray or variegated companion as a foil. Also, may be floppy, so a peony cage is a good idea.

ZONES 3–9

Clematis rehderiana ▾

deciduous vine

Big, scented, floriferous, long bloom season: what more good can I say to convince you? This Chinese native (commonly known as nodding virgin's bower, or cowslip-scented clematis) makes a case for itself wherever it grows. Yes, it gets a bit heavy, but it flowers on the new growth and can be hard pruned every year. The flowers look like little barristers' wigs from the English judicial courts, in a yummy buttery yellow. Hummingbirds have learned that anything so deliciously perfumed (strongly of primroses) has great nectar.

HEIGHT 16.5–23 feet (5–7 m)
LIGHT EXPOSURE Full sun.
PRUNING Hard prune in the winter or early spring. Flowers on the new and old growth, but it gets so big in one year that pruning by at least half is the way to go.
BLOOM TIME Mid-June through late September, continuous without deadheading. New growth comes into bloom as the early growth wanes.
LANDSCAPE USE Want to cover a cyclone fence with something that smells great? This is it. Also makes a lovely backdrop for colorful herbaceous perennials.
ZONES 6–9

Clematis 'Roguchi' ▸

herbaceous perennial

This astounding vine is often listed in the Integrifolia Group, but it is so different from its fellows, I'm placing it with "other." This is not intended to be damning with faint praise; quite the opposite. This is the only widely known cross involving *Clematis integrifolia* that brought forth a climbing plant. The other parent was *C. reticulata* from North America (obviously the breeder was thinking more about creating a unique cut flower than a vine for garden worthiness). When the plant was brought into the trade by Joy Creek Nursery, it was discovered that it will climb, reaching at least half its length by the usual manner before turning its attention to flowering. Not able to multitask, once 'Roguchi' comes into bloom, it loses interest in climbing and folds over itself. The blossoms are exquisite deep blue straight-sided bells, with lighter margins.

HEIGHT 6–7 feet (1.8–2 m)
LIGHT EXPOSURE Full sun, six hours a day or more. Anything less makes the leaves susceptible to mildew.
PRUNING Since this is at heart an herbaceous perennial, hard pruning down to a few inches tall after dormancy in late autumn or winter is a necessity. All new growth comes from the base. None of the top growth will regenerate to bloom the next year. If it should get mildew in the spring, cut it back and make it start over.
BLOOM TIME May and June. Cut back by half its length after flowering (or hard prune again) to spur a second flowering in late summer, usually from late August into the autumn.
LANDSCAPE USE Best used draping down a retaining wall, or climbing upward into a not terribly dense large shrub. The bells are beautiful punctuating the autumn colors of Japanese maples.
ZONES 4–9

Clematis 'Royal Velours' ▾

Viticella Group, deciduous vine

Arguably the darkest of any red clematis, the color is dramatic and perhaps slightly hard to place. This is another of the French Morel hybrids introduced through England after a sojourn at Gravetye Manor. In full sun, the color will be dark red in the style of 'Niobe'. In overcast weather or partial shade, it will be more like the color of very fine Bordeaux.

HEIGHT 10.5–13 feet (3–4 m)

LIGHT EXPOSURE Mid- to full sun; especially fine in hot afternoon sun. Shaded roots preferred, but with enough water, it will tolerate sun from the ground up.

PRUNING Hard prune to 1 foot (30 cm) in late winter.

BLOOM TIME After hard pruning in winter, flowers in July/August. This plant responds well to manip-ulation of standard pruning advice. If pruned by one-half its length after the first wave of bloom, it will rebloom from autumn to frost in temperate climates.

LANDSCAPE USE At Kinzy Faire, a garden outside Estacada, Oregon, this vine is grown to great effect in *Cornus controversa* 'Variegata'. Also effective on metalwork handrails or similar low woven border edging, where the flowers may be admired closely.

ZONES 4–10

Clematis 'Ruby'

Atragene Group, deciduous vine

'Ruby' is still the reddest of the widely available Atragene Group hybrids. Although the color is a hue or two lighter than ruby red, in cooler climates the color is truly gem-like. This form is double, and the flowering time quite early, sometimes in late March. This fine cultivar was not only named but developed by William Robinson's head gardener at Gravetye Manor, Ernest Markham.

HEIGHT 6.5–13 feet (2–4 m)
LIGHT EXPOSURE Mid- to full sun. Shaded roots preferred, and gravel rather than organic mulch.
PRUNING Prune as needed after the first wave of blooms is spent, giving the vine the remainder of the growing season to recover. In areas with very cold winters, do not remove the old leaves as they curl around the nodes. This is probably an adaptation to the cold, protecting the latent buds in the node for the coming year.
BLOOM TIME Early April through early May with good rebloom in 60–90 days.
LANDSCAPE USE Very pretty combined with hedging such as *Viburnum tinus*, which flowers at the same time.
ZONES 3–8

Clematis 'Sir Trevor Lawrence'

Texensis Group, herbaceous vine

Need a splashy sun-loving vine with unusually shaped flowers? Want to be the envy of your neighbors? Then you want this plant. Imagine the rich red of 'Gravetye Beauty' but with more substance and a hot violet bar within the lily-flowered-tulip–shaped blooms. And to think, this cultivar was lost for 75 years until a robust old specimen was spotted by Christopher Lloyd, who had sense enough to know what he was seeing and bring it back into the trade.

HEIGHT 6.5–9 feet (2–3 m)
LIGHT EXPOSURE Best with sun from the ground up, all day.
PRUNING Hard prune in the winter or early spring. There is little rejuvenation of the upper vines, and it is better to let the whole thing start over every year.
BLOOM TIME Mid-June through late September, continuous without deadheading.
LANDSCAPE USE Great with fellow sun-lovers such as rock-roses (*Cistus*) and large penstemons, good in rock gardens and in roses.
ZONES 4–9

Clematis 'Sizaia Ptitsa'

Integrifolia Group, herbaceous perennial

By any other name, this clematis would sell better. It is a luscious, more purple relation of *Clematis ×durandii* (a child of it, actually) and deserves to be planted everywhere, in many different garden applications. Alas, the name flummoxes people. According to Brewster Rogerson, who spit liberally when he said it, "If you don't get any on you, you're not saying it right." Debbie Fischer of Silver Star Vinery has reduced it to "slice-a-pizza," which seems to work as well as anything.

HEIGHT 4–6.5 feet (1.2–2 m)
LIGHT EXPOSURE Full sun, six hours a day or more.
PRUNING Since this is an herbaceous perennial plant, hard pruning down to a few inches tall after dormancy in late autumn or winter is a necessity. All new growth comes from the base.
BLOOM TIME May and June. Cut back by half its length after flowering (or hard prune again) to spur a second flowering in late summer, usually from late August into the autumn.
LANDSCAPE USE Once you've accepted the fact that it doesn't climb, you can do anything with this plant: groundcover, rose companion, hydrangea pal (I have mine with *Hydrangea macrophylla* 'Nigra'), herbaceous perennial pairings, you name it. It will be more compact for being cut back hard at midsummer.
ZONES 3–9

Clematis terniflora

deciduous vine

Clematis terniflora (sweet autumn clematis) has undergone a shocking number of name changes, but this one seems to have stuck. Many nurseries still mistakenly label it *C. paniculata*, which is native to New Zealand (not Japan) and is actually completely different (not fall blooming or particularly fragrant). Like *C. flammula*, *C. terniflora* may take a few years to develop its fragrance if you've purchased seed-grown plants. Well-established plants are the most highly scented. Produces frothy masses of tiny white flowers. Warning: in the southeastern United States, this plant reseeds so rampantly, it has landed itself on noxious weed lists. In many places in the South, it is now a prohibited plant. Needs cold winters and long damp cool springs to kill the seeds or rot the seedlings.

HEIGHT up to 30 feet (9 m), easily, in one year
LIGHT EXPOSURE Full sun, or it will not bloom in cool-summer climates.
PRUNING Hard prune in the winter or early spring. It will get huge if you don't.
BLOOM TIME In hot summers, it might start as early as August. In the Pacific Northwest, expect a great October show.
LANDSCAPE USE Best on strong built structures of wrought iron or heavy lumber.
ZONES 5–11

Clematis texensis

deciduous vine

Commonly known as the scarlet lady, or scarlet leather flower, this is the one and true Holy Grail species for clematis collectors. Although native to Texas, it was in France in the 1890s that this vine made a name for itself as the pollen or seed parent in the hybridization of more truly red large-flowered hybrids. There are two acknowledged naturally occurring variants. The elongated urns of the form growing in the Tarpley River area are red both inside and out. This is considered the best form for hybridization. From the wild areas of Travis County around Austin, Texas, comes a form with a more plump, egg or bonnet shape, red or coral on the outside and cream to yellow on the margins and interior sepal surfaces. This vine too has great éclat. Both are pollinated in the wild by ruby-throated hummingbirds. In the rest of the United States, other hummingbird species recognize food when they see it in gardens.

HEIGHT 6–7 feet (1.8–2 m)
LIGHT EXPOSURE Full sun, but with ample water and good drainage.
PRUNING Hard prune in the winter or early spring. There is little rejuvenation of the upper vines, and it is better to let the whole thing start over every year.
BLOOM TIME Late June through late autumn, continuous with deadheading (but who in their right mind would sacrifice the seed production!).
LANDSCAPE USE Lovely grown over low mounding rockroses (*Cistus*) and other sun-loving summer shrubs, or in gravel gardens. It is content to be as much groundcover as vertical climber.
ZONES 4–9

Clematis tubulosa Alan Bloom 'Alblo'

Heracleifolia Group, deciduous subshrub

One of the most floriferous of this durable group, with slender mid-blue bells that split and curl back as the florets mature. In difficult sites (hot sun, high desert/steppe climates), this subshrub will become a dense drought-tolerant summer bloomer. In more luxurious temperate climates, it will spread by self-layering and can become invasive. A beautiful thug, but a thug nonetheless . . . Mildly fragrant. Named by Blooms of Bressingham for their founder.

HEIGHT 2–4 feet (0.5–1.2 m) and about as wide

LIGHT EXPOSURE Mid- to full sun; especially fine in hot afternoon sun.

PRUNING Hard prune to 1 foot (30 cm) in late winter/early spring, once emerging buds become obvious.

BLOOM TIME Flowers in July/August when many other clematis are resting.

LANDSCAPE USE Effective in swaths amongst ornamental grasses and late summer herbaceous perennials such as heleniums, rudbeckias, and the various perennial sunflowers (*Helianthus*).

ZONES 3–11

Clematis 'Venosa Violacea' ❄

Viticella Group, deciduous vine

After growing clematis for 30 years (got the first one when I was ten . . . I can see you doing the math, you know), this is still The One. The parentage is *viticella* × *florida*. *Clematis viticella* donates the texture with violet veining and outline; from *C. florida* comes the white self color and form—opening flat and upfacing—and the dark anthers. But unlike so many sports of and hybrids involving *C. florida*, 'Venosa Violacea' is not capricious. This is a sturdy, durable, adaptable, elegant vine. When glimpsed in *Clematis* (Fretwell 1989), it was love at first sight.

HEIGHT 6.5–13 feet (2–4 m)
LIGHT EXPOSURE Mid- to full sun; especially fine in hot afternoon sun. Shaded roots preferred, but with enough water, it will tolerate sun from the ground up. The flower color will vary from the shady to the sunny side of the plant; shade brings out the purple with a wider margin and sun highlights the violet.
PRUNING Hard prune to 1 foot (30 cm) in late winter.
BLOOM TIME After hard pruning in winter, flowers in July/August. This plant responds well to manipulation of standard pruning advice. If pruned by one-half its length after the first wave of bloom, it will rebloom from autumn to frost in temperate climates.
LANDSCAPE USE Elegance enhances elegance. I have placed this clematis with my favorite rose, 'Sombreuil'. The climbing rose starts earlier in the growing season, but by mid-June the duet begins and continues all summer, with solo interludes by each. This clematis also performs very well with others in the Viticella Group and, fellow sun-worshipers, the Texensis Group.
ZONES 5–10

Clematis 'Warwickshire Rose' ❄

Montana Group, deciduous vine

I consider this to be the finest of the pink Montana Group selections. The milleflorous blooms are cotton-candy pink outlined with a darker margin, giving the whole vine a rosy appearance. The foliage speaks as well of the plant as the flowers do, holding its bronze-red color throughout a longer season than most of this heritage. Not much fragrance.

HEIGHT 16.5–30 feet (5–9 m)
LIGHT EXPOSURE Mid- to full sun. If planted in partial shade, the plant will seek the amount of sun it requires to bloom well.
PRUNING Prune to whatever degree necessary in late June, after flowering. This gives the plant the growing season to recover enough to flower on time the next year. Many in the Montana Group benefit from a rejuvenating hard pruning every 3–5 years.
BLOOM TIME May well into June. Some modest, random rebloom in August.
LANDSCAPE USE Useful wherever a large showy vine is wanted, especially on a flat-panel trellis where you will have a wall of rosy pink. Most cultivars in this group become large and quite heavy-trunked over time—plan accordingly for ample support.
ZONES 7–10

Clematis 'White Swan'

Atragene Group, deciduous vine

There are many good white cultivars in the Atragene Group. This hybrid is presented here because it is the most widely available. There is a sparkle to the double white flowers, reminding one of snowflakes. As a rule, the whites do not rebloom as well as some of the other colors in this group. This may be due to the influence of *Clematis sibirica*, the species that brings white to this group: it does not rebloom well, but it is the hardiest clematis on earth.

HEIGHT 6.5–16.5 feet (2–5 m)

LIGHT EXPOSURE Mid- to full sun. Shaded roots preferred, and gravel rather than organic mulch.

PRUNING Prune as needed after the first wave of blooms is spent, giving the vine the remainder of the growing season to recover. In areas with very cold winters, do not remove the old leaves as they curl around the nodes. This is probably an adaptation to the cold, protecting the latent buds in the node for the coming year.

BLOOM TIME Mid-April through mid-May with good rebloom in 60–90 days.

LANDSCAPE USE Makes an attractive textural accent with small-leafed broadleaf evergreens, such as variegated boxwood. Also lovely combined with blue, and especially with lower-growing varieties of California lilac (*Ceanothus*). Good tumbling down a retaining wall, too.

ZONES 3–9

GROWING
AND
PROPAGATING

If you are an average gardener but have never grown clematis, you will find their needs not much different from other plants. So let's start at the beginning, selecting and planting your new clematis, and move along from there.

Selecting and Planting

Most clematis are sold in what in America are called 1-gallon or #1 pots, roughly 5 inches (12 cm) wide and 8 inches (20 cm) deep. Affixed to the pot is a 3-foot (1-m) hardwood or bamboo stake, and the clematis is tied to it (whether it is a climber or not!). Check the drainage holes for roots, remembering that a clematis slightly pot-bound is likely a stronger specimen than one with a meager amount of roots. Next, look at the number of shoots coming from the surface of the soil. Any number greater than one is preferable to a vine with all its growth dependent on a lone stem. If you have the choice of a vine with multiple shoots but no flower buds and the same cultivar with only one shoot but several buds, choose the multi-stemmed specimen. When young, the root system vigor and numerous shoots are a better indicator of health than a mass of leaves and buds.

If you buy a plant mail-order that arrives bare-rooted, or in a pot smaller than just described, *do not* put the plant in the ground immediately. This point cannot be overstated. Would you leave a child in the woods to fend for itself? No. Therefore, if you must buy a small clematis to get the cultivar you want, plant it into a 1-gallon pot until it has formed a strong root system. This may take a month or two, or a year. In any case, you are giving the plant a head start by allowing the root system to become well established.

Clematis heracleifolia 'Cassandra' (Heracleifolia Group) at the Rogerson Clematis Garden. Like every other clematis, it was thoroughly moistened at planting time, but like any of this group, it is drought tolerant once established.

Clematis may be planted anytime as long as the ground is not frozen, soggy, or bone dry. Start by digging a hole 18 inches (45 cm) deep and several inches wider than the pot the clematis is in. Remove any supporting stake from the pot, and if it is a vining type of clematis, prune it to 15–18 inches (38–45 cm) tall when you plant it. This greatly reduces transplant shock. It also makes the plant easier to handle as you seat it in its planting hole. I fully understand you don't want to prune at planting—it seems counterintuitive. But it is much, *much* better for your climbing clematis to be pruned at planting time. No matter how careful you are as you transplant, feeder roots will be damaged, reducing the plant's ability to support all that length of leafy vine the nurseryman left on the clematis to make it appear more saleable. *Prune when you plant*. Period.

As you are digging your deep hole, allow the clematis (still in its pot or out of it) to soak in a deep tub of water until the root ball stops bubbling. You want your new clematis to be thoroughly moistened at planting time.

Once your hole is dug, throw some organic compost or composted manure into the bottom, along with a handful of either bone meal or organic rose and flower food. If you are planting a clematis in the Atragene, Texensis,

Clematis 'Jenny' (Montana Group) is supported by a sturdy post and hog wire.

or Evergreen (New Zealand) Groups, add a cup of No. 2 chicken grit or quarter-ten (washed) gravel into the hole to add extra drainage. Mix this all together with some of your native garden soil. Fill the hole by half with water and let it drain. Now the hole is ready for the clematis.

If you are planting a large-flowered hybrid, bury the bottom 2–3 inches (5–7.5 cm) of the vine as you plant it (assuming there are growth nodes). If the lowest nodes are higher than this, plant the clematis deeper, so the lowest nodes are buried by a couple of inches of soil, or mulch them afterward. **No** other types of clematis should be buried, *only* large-flowered hybrids. *Every other type* of clematis should be planted at the same level in the ground as it was in the pot in which it was purchased.

Got that? Bury the bottom stems of large-flowered hybrids, but **not** the other kinds.

Once the clematis is sitting at the proper level, backfill the hole with good garden soil with some compost mixed into it. Firm the soil around the clematis roots as you go without pushing down on the stems. Once you have the hole filled and the clematis is secure you may slide the stake it came with into the soil (don't stab the crown of the clematis . . . that would be bad) at an angle to guide the vines into a host plant or onto a built structure. This may not be necessary, given your plant's particular situation.

To review selecting and planting:

- Choose a specimen with roots showing at the drainage holes and multiple shoots at the soil surface.
- General vigor is more important than whether it is about to bloom.
- If the clematis is small or bare-rooted, plant into a pot to allow roots to develop before planting in the ground.
- **Prune** vining clematis when you plant them. Don't scalp them to the ground, but do take them back to 15–18 inches (38–45 cm) tall. **Just do it.**
- Water well at planting time. Soak the root ball and the planting hole.
- Amend the soil in the planting hole with compost and organic rose and flower food or bone meal. Adjust for drainage by adding grit or gravel.
- Bury the bottom 2–3 inches (5–7.5 cm) of the vine if the clematis is a large-flowered hybrid only. *Do not bury the other forms.*
- Place any guiding stakes near the clematis crown.

Tip: planting clematis under an established tree

If the roots of the tree are so dense you cannot dig a decent hole, or if siting the clematis at the drip line of the tree canopy would be awkward, knock the bottom out of a big pot, place the pot where you want the clematis to be, and plant the clematis into the pot. Eventually the clematis roots will fill the pot and find their own way down into the soil amongst the tree roots. This is especially effective when planting clematis into fruit trees.

Siting Your Clematis

"Feet in the shade, head in the sun" is a charming gener-
alization, but it does not apply more than about half the
time. Some clematis tolerate partial shade and are prettier
for it, and some want sun from the ground up to thrive and
flower well. This particular old wives' tale comes from the
assumption that shaded soil is more moisture retentive
(if you have dry shade, you know what a lie *that* is), and
clematis like to be evenly moist. The following sections on
sun- and shade-preferring clematis will confirm just how
adaptable clematis can be.

CLEMATIS FOR BRIGHT EXPOSURES

While it is generally true that most large-flowered hybrids
prefer six or more hours of sun a day, there are a few that
simply will *not* bloom well without much more light than
that. The red and purple large-flowered hybrids want as
much light as possible. Within the large-flowered hybrids
is a subgroup heavily influenced by *Clematis florida* and *C.
viticella*; they *must* have full sun and summer warmth, or
over time they will dwindle away. While there are a few
double large-flowered hybrids on the low-light list, all will
be more vigorous and produce more flowers in full sun.
The doubles are too numerous to list here; simply assume
they are a "yes" to the sun.

Amongst the small-flowered groups, there are several
we can treat as unabashed sun-worshippers. The Texensis, Integrifolia, and Tangutica/Orientalis Groups will
require as much light and warmth as possible during the
growing season and will not bloom well without it. The
Viticella Group loves the sun but can tolerate less light,
at least for the time it takes to mount their growth into a
small tree and reach the sun at its top.

C. 'Andromeda' (white/red bar)
C. 'Barbara Dibley' (pink/red bar)
C. Bijou 'Evipo030' (lavender)
C. Bourbon 'Evipo018' (red/pink bar)
C. 'Candida' (white)
C. 'Comtesse de Bouchaud' (pink)
C. 'Danuta' (pink)
C. 'Ernest Markham' (red)
C. 'Fond Memories' (white/red outline)
C. 'Henryi' (white)
C. 'Iubileinyi-70' (purple)
C. 'Jackmanii' (purple)
C. 'Kacper' (purple)
C. Kingfisher 'Evipo037' (lavender-blue)
C. 'Lady Betty Balfour' (purple)
C. 'Madame Baron-Veillard' (pink)
C. 'Negritianka' (purple)
C. 'Omoshiro' (white/red outline)
C. 'Perle d'Azur' (blue)
C. 'Piilu' Little Duckling (pink/red bar)
C. Rebecca 'Evipo016' (red)
C. 'Rhapsody' (blue)
C. Rosemoor 'Evipo002' (red)
C. 'Rouge Cardinal' (red)
C. 'Victoria' (purple)
C. 'Ville de Lyon' (red)
C. Wisley 'Evipo001' (purple)

Sun-worshippers: *Clematis* Wisley 'Evipo001' (Large-flowered Hybrid) with C. 'Bill MacKenzie' (Tangutica/Orientalis Group).

Clematis 'Perrin's Pride'
(Large-flowered Hybrid) drapes
along a shaded retaining wall.

C. 'Asao' (pink)

C. 'Barbara Jackman' (lavender/red bar)

C. 'Bees' Jubilee' (pink/red bar)

C. 'Blue Ravine' (lavender-blue)

C. 'Candy Stripe' (lavender/red bar)

C. 'Daniel Deronda' (purple-blue)

C. 'Doctor Ruppel' (pink/red bar)

C. 'Edomurasaki' Blue Bird (purple)

C. 'Fair Rosamond' (beige)

C. 'Fujimusume' (blue)

C. 'Gillian Blades' (white)

C. 'Hakuokan' (purple)

C. 'Honora' (plum)

C. 'King Edward VII' (lavender-stippled pink)

C. 'Louise Rowe' (blue, double)

C. 'Lady Northcliffe' (lavender-blue)

C. 'Mrs. George Jackman' (white)

C. 'Nelly Moser' (pink/red bar)

C. 'Niobe' (red)

C. 'Perrin's Pride' (purple)

C. 'Peveril Pearl' (lavender)

C. 'Pinky' (pink/red bar)

C. 'Semu' (purple)

C. 'Solidarnosc' (red)

C. 'Teshio' (lavender-blue, double)

C. 'Tsuzuki' (white)

C. Vancouver 'Morning Mist' (pink)

C. 'Veronica's Choice' (lavender, double)

C. 'Vyvyan Pennell' (mauve/blue, double)

C. 'Warszawska Nike' Midnight Showers (plum)

C. 'Warszawska Olga' (pink)

C. 'Will Barron' (lavender-blue)

C. 'Will Goodwin' (lavender-blue)

CLEMATIS FOR LOW-LIGHT EXPOSURES

If you know a clematis is a woodland species, or is bred from a woodland species (many large-flowered hybrids have the woodland marginal *Clematis patens* in their lineage), it will tolerate partial shade readily. This is where it truly is handy to know how plants grow in the wild.

Many of the barred large-flowered hybrids tolerate partial shade well, and the lower light keeps their colors bright as the flowers age. Most clematis with subtle colors appreciate partial shade.

Evergreen clematis related to *Clematis armandii* and *C. montana* forms will grow well in partial shade, but the lower several feet of vine will become trunky and leafless without sunlight reaching down to preserve lower leaves. Woody lower vines can lend a garden the appearance of maturity, but some folks simply do not like vines with bare lower legs. Choose accordingly.

Clematis 'Semu' (Large-flowered Hybrid) glows in a shady ensemble.

Pruning

If only we could start over with the entire history of pruning clematis . . . There are ongoing international discussions about how to reinvent pruning instructions for the genus *Clematis*, happening at a snail's pace. That gardeners have come to judge the garden-worthiness of a clematis based on how it is pruned is maddening. It makes one rude sometimes. Yes, some people prefer having hard and fast rules. But clematis can't read. They just grow and flower as the season and opportunity allow. Perhaps rather than rules, we might have suggestions. We cannot hope to simplify this complicated genus, but we can *clarify* and agree to some simple terminology that helps it all make sense. So, let's do a little myth-busting:

- Group One: Clematis that *must* not be pruned. Ha! There is no such thing as a clematis that doesn't need some type of pruning, sometime.
- Group Two: Clematis that *must* be pruned by some arcane formula and at a time of year that is kept vague, to preserve older stems that will produce the largest and most double flowers.
- Group Three: Clematis that *must* be hard pruned to nearly the ground every single year or they will grow forever and ever and soon be flowering in neighboring counties.

Ugh. If we look at the three groups and remove the word "must" from each, substituting the word "may," we come a bit closer to the truth of how clematis grow, and how most right-thinking gardeners actually prune them.

The clematis groups relegated to Group One typically bloom in early spring (March/April). Traditionally this has included the Montana and Atragene Groups, as well as the Evergreen (Armandii) Group and winter-flowering clematis. Many of these clematis become huge, or at least heavy, with age. It is important that they be revitalized with sometimes quite severe pruning to keep the old wood from wearing out. In the case of the Atragenes, if they are grown in long-season climates, they may rebloom, which can complicate things further. So let's suggest the following: Group One are clematis that, when they are pruned, are reduced by at least half of their mature length immediately after their initial flowering period. This may be done every year (for the Atragene and

There are no clematis that never need pruning. This specimen of *Clematis* 'Jacqueline du Pré' (Atragene Group) may be pruned immediately after flowering.

When you do prune, cut back to just above a pair of good buds.

Cirrhosa [winter-flowering] Groups), every other year (for the Montana and Cirrhosa [winter-flowering] Groups), or every five years (for the Montana and Evergreen [Armandii] Groups), depending on how the plant is used in a garden. Yes, there is overlap. And as has been mentioned, in some cases (like the Evergreen [Armandii] Group), regular pruning is good garden hygiene. Just be sure you prune these early in the growing season, immediately after flowering, to give the vines ample time to produce new growth throughout the summer so they will bloom on time the next year.

Group Two is meant to address those in the Large-flowered Hybrid Group that flower biggest on the previous year's growth, allegedly. This entire construct has been disproved. Consider Kansas, or any part of the interior of North America. Given the severe winters common to the continental climate, the only option with the Large-flowered Hybrid Group is to hard prune them *all*—late, early, and indifferent—down to 6–12 inches (15–30 cm) tall in late winter. That much dies every year, yet back the clematis come, blooming boisterously a bit later than their coastal counterparts, with every bit of their size and rude good health. Spring arrives quick and warm, so the vines grow rapidly once they start, and those capable of producing broad blossoms, 8–10 inches (20–25 cm) wide, rush to do so. This explains why such cultivars as 'Henryi' are better plants for the Midwest than the Pacific Northwest, where springs can be halting.

For regions where such severe dieback is unlikely but freezing is still common, go look at your clematis sometime after the end of January. Your large-flowered hybrids will show you exactly where their next growth will occur by inflating the buds at the nodes. You might need to observe carefully, as the buds may be reddish brown at first rather than bright green, but they will develop rapidly once the days get longer, and you need only cut off dead growth and live wood back to where the buds are plumpest. Don't follow a formula, don't figure a third or a half—in fact, avoid fractions altogether. Just observe the vine, find the live nodes, and cut off what seems excessive, always making your cuts right above a pair of likely-looking buds. If you don't get to it until April, growth will have started, and if you are a timid pruner, you may not take off as much old growth as you could, but the worst that will happen is your clematis will flower later in the season.

There are many clematis that benefit from annual hard pruning, but few that truly must be pruned down to 12 inches (30 cm) tall or less every year. The Integrifolia Group, being herbaceous perennials, must be cleaned up in the winter. The Viorna Group, particularly the Texensis Group, are mainly herbaceous vines, with little or no new growth coming from the previous year's vines. Good garden hygiene suggests clearing out the old vines as soon as they go dormant in late autumn or winter.

Clematis 'Huvi' (Large-flowered Hybrid) is best pruned back to a pair of strong buds in late winter/early spring every year.

"Iva Biggun," or the largest of the large-flowered hybrids

UNBEKNOWNST TO THEM, EVERY SPRING the clematis at the Rogerson Clematis Garden engage in a contest. Who amongst them will produce the broadest blossom? For those of you for whom size matters, or who have a competitive nature, here is the list of clematis featured in this book that have won the contest or come close.

Clematis Vancouver 'Morning Mist' (Large-flowered Hybrid), the grand champion, measures up at a whopping 11 inches (28 cm) wide.

C. 'Barbara Dibley' (pink/red bar)
C. Bourbon 'Evipo018' (red/pink bar)
C. 'Candida' (white)
C. 'Frau Mikiko' (purple)
C. 'Gillian Blades' (white)
C. 'Henryi' (white)
C. 'King George V' (pink)
C. 'Kacper' (purple)
C. 'Omoshiro' (white/red outline)
C. 'Peveril Pearl' (lavender)
C. 'Pinky' (pink/red bar)
C. Vancouver 'Morning Mist' (pink)
C. 'W. E. Gladstone' (lavender-blue)

Oxymoron: smaller large-flowered hybrids

THERE ARE THOSE WHO MIGHT THINK the largest clematis flowers somewhat tawdry. The average width for most flowers in this group is about 6 inches (15 cm). Very large might be considered anything over 8 inches (20 cm) in breadth, and small would be 5 inches (12 cm) or less. If they are that small, why still include them in the Large-flowered Hybrid Group? It has to do with the poise of the flower (out- or upfacing), parentage, and the vine's growth habit and bloom time. If it behaves like a large-flowered hybrid and is bred from large-flowered hybrids, then it is one, regardless of average flower size.

Keep in mind: just because the flowers are small, it does not follow that the vine will be of petite stature.

C. Alaina 'Evipo056' (pink)
C. 'Barbara Jackman' (lavender/red bar)
C. Bijou 'Evipo030' (lavender)
C. 'Blue Eyes' (blue)
C. 'Comtesse de Bouchaud' (pink)
C. Fleuri 'Evipo042' (purple)
C. Jackmanii Purpurea 'Zojapur' (purple)
C. 'Negritianka' (purple)
C. 'Piilu' Little Duckling (pink/red bar)
C. 'Rhapsody' (blue)
C. 'Tsuzuki' (white)

Clematis 'Piilu' Little Duckling (Large-flowered Hybrid) in a coastal garden. Its group designation notwithstanding, the flowers of 'Piilu', although always generously produced, are on a more human scale, a mere 3–5 inches (7.5–12 cm) wide.

The interesting thing about the supposed "late" large-flowered hybrids is that if left to their own devices, they are not late! If left unpruned through the winter, they will bloom in May. So, with cultivars such as 'Jackmanii' and its descendants, it is far from necessary to hard prune in the winter. It works perfectly well to allow this group to flower early before hard pruning them *after* their first flowers have faded. In long-season climates, they will rebloom in late summer or autumn.

The Viticella Group is generally disposed to flower later than any of the large-flowered hybrids whether pruned or not, and they usually rebloom if their length is reduced by half after their July sepals have dropped. Hard pruning in winter does ensure more shoots burst from the ground, but if you want a vine from this group to be large, by all means forgo pruning and let it ramble high and wide for a year or two without hindrance.

Where does that leave us? Perhaps, ultimately, we might do away with Group Two completely. We could have only Group One, those clematis that may be pruned by half or more when it is needed, most usually when they are done flowering the first time in the growing season. And Group Three—which will become Group Two—will be the clematis that should always be hard pruned. Oh, there will be outrage, and everyone will swear they have the exception that proves me wrong, but really, it could all be much simpler if we judge clematis by how they actually grow, rather than by any rigid notion of rules.

Clematis 'Buckland Beauty' (Viorna Group) is an herbaceous vine. Not much of it rejuvenates from year to year, making hard pruning in the winter, each winter, the logical maintenance choice.

Forgetting to prune *Clematis* 'Viola' (Large-flowered Hybrid) in the winter one year taught me it would bloom with roses in May. It is hard pruned after the May blossoms are spent, for autumn rebloom.

Clematis 'Chatsworth' (Viticella Group) benefits from annual winter hard pruning.

Tidying or Hard-deadheading

If you choose to deadhead your large-flowered hybrids after their first wave of bloom in the spring, you can take the opportunity to tidy the clematis, or what is called hard-deadheading. This means taking off more than just the seedhead. Perhaps the clematis has wandered into a rose and is flowering prettily, but you worry that the final 2–3 feet (0.5–1 m) of the clematis is more than you want the rose to bear. If you're taking off the spent blossom to encourage rebloom anyway, why not cut off the offending length of vine at the same time? Fertilize after this tidying, and the vine will branch at the next node below where you cut it, producing two new stems, and you may expect rebloom in 30–45 days.

If you hard-deadhead herbaceous perennial clematis, the new shoots will come from the crown rather than branching where they were cut, but the result is the same. If you fertilize when you deadhead (taking off extra length if you want), expect rebloom rapidly.

New shoots emerging from the crown of the herbaceous perennial *Clematis mandshurica*.

Providing Structure

Simply put, do not underestimate the sturdiness required of a built structure for clematis, especially if multiple plants will be supported. The first structure shown here has a clematis on each post, but one of them, the abundantly blooming *Clematis montana* var. *wilsonii* hort. is a galloping vine, which will span all four corners of the structure in time. The structure was planned for this eventuality.

In other instances it is only necessary to provide vertical guidance for a lighter-weight vine, especially if it houses a clematis to be hard pruned in the winter. If it is to be freestanding, make sure it has anchors reaching well into the ground for sufficient stability.

Words to live by: no bare posts! And if one has the opportunity to multitask with an upright structure, so much the better. Young clematis will be unable to reach around a post that is 4 × 4 inches (10 × 10 cm) to pull

Structures destined to hold several clematis must be sturdy. Clematis are not as destructive as other vines, but don't underestimate their weight!

Clematis 'Princess Diana' (Texensis Group) on an iron structure. Sometimes a structure needs to contain as much as support.

themselves up; but surround a birdhouse or weathervane post with chicken wire or fencing cloth, and any climbing clematis will know what to do.

Generally speaking, clematis should be provided as many points of contact as possible as they climb. Thin chicken wire or fencing cloth, thicker hog wire (with larger openings), heavier cement reinforcement panels, and structures made of half-inch (1.25 cm) rebar all work admirably to reduce wind breakage.

Fencing cloth is a boon to clematis. It may be purchased in rolls 25, 50, or 100 feet (7.5, 15, or 30 m) in length and 2–4 feet (0.5–1.2 m) wide. It can be used to fill in the space between side rails and across supports of upright flat-panel structures and attached all the way around the back side of the structure. Posts can be topped with finials to protect from rain seepage into the cut surface; metal, wood, and glass caps for posts that are 4 × 4 inches (10 × 10 cm) are widely available, and artists make pottery versions.

Ever wonder what hog wire is? *Clematis* 'Stasik' (Large-flowered Hybrid) on hog wire fencing.

Clematis Golden Tiara 'Kugotia' (Tangutica/Orientalis Group) easily makes its way up this wire-covered post.

Common Pests and Diseases

THE "W" WORD—WILT

Let's get this unsavory topic out of the way with all possible haste. Large-flowered hybrid clematis, especially those most closely related to *Clematis patens*, are the only clematis widely grown that are likely to fall prey to the fungus *Phoma clematidina*, the pathogen behind clematis wilt, or juvenile wilt disease. This fungal infection is spread through the air and typically affects young clematis by entering the stems through wounds and breaks. The disease follows a typical progression, often striking, quite diabolically, when the clematis are already stressed because they are about to bloom. The buds and tip growth start to nod, as if they need water. They do! The fungus disrupts the flow of water in the plant's vascular system, which carries water up the vines. You water the clematis, but it does not perk up.

The fungus spreads rapidly throughout the top growth of the vine. Within days, the *entire* plant has gone limp, and within a week, it has turned black. Cut the plant back to the ground immediately. Fertilize the crown, and hope for the best. The spores do not spread underground, or in water. This is why burying a few lower nodes underground at planting time is important for the large-flowered hybrids. New shoots should emerge from the crown in 30–45 days, but it might take longer. The infected top growth you have removed should be placed in a garbage sack and put out with the trash. Do not add it to yard debris cans (it is rude to pass along your gardening problems), and do not try to compost the remains—most likely your composting system does not get hot enough to kill the spores. Do not use fungicides, including those labeled "organic," as even mild fungicides have been linked to bee colony collapse.

The name "wilt" is unfortunate, as many things can cause a clematis to droop suddenly: lack of water, failing to prune the new vine when it is planted, slug and snail damage to the lower stems, breakage at the lower nodes, fertilizing heavily when the plant is about to bloom. If your plant is growing horizontally, and you decide you want it to head upright, you will often break the stem at the connecting node as you tie it up, so the next day you go out and the freshly tied stem has collapsed. That's not wilt disease; that is operator error. Stems growing horizontally want to stay that way. If the sideways stems are a bother, cut them back.

Peter Skeggs-Gooch, third-generation nurseryman at Thorncroft Clematis in Norfolk, England, maintains that most of what is thought to be juvenile wilt disease is actually slug or snail damage. In addition to feeding on the flowers, these pests love to eat the lower bark on young clematis stems, and if they eat all the way around a stem (girdling), the stem will collapse. Therefore, if you have a plant with only a couple of limp stems, look for slug damage, and apply organic slug bait around the crown of the plant.

Wilt is not the only fungal disease of clematis. Many of the dark-flowered forms can attract powdery mildew, especially as the flowers decline. This is common in 'Viola' and 'Romantika', two dramatic dark large-flowered hybrids bred in Estonia. When the first wave of spring and early summer bloom goes into decline, white spots form on the sepals, which may eventually turn the entire flower an unfortunate gray-white. For this reason I have not included these two cultivars in the plant directory.

Slug damage on flowers; note the shiny slime at upper left.

There is hope. Make sure these and other similarly susceptible varieties (the leaves of 'Roguchi' can also be afflicted) are grown in full sun. As soon as mildew appears over about a third of the plant, cut it down to the ground and fertilize it. If the clematis has a healthy root system, it will bounce back quickly and rebloom later in the summer when the weather is hot. It is unlikely the plants will be as beset in hotter weather.

OTHER CRETINOUS CRITTERS

Slugs are a serious clematis pest, but they are not the only invertebrates that find new shoots toothsome. Watch out for earwigs. This insect pest shreds leaves and flowers nocturnally. Often a discrete hole appears in the side of a clematis bud; when the bud opens the truth is exposed: the innards have been eaten out of the flower and the sepals are shredded. Sometimes the earwig is still there, revealed for the scoundrel it is.

The other nasty creature of the night is the cutworm (army worm), a plump, brown, tan, or green caterpillar (1 inch/2.5 cm long, more or less) that feeds at night on new shoots, specializing in chewing through tender stems just below the flower buds. Nothing is more disheartening of a garden morning than to come upon the evidence of these marauders' activity, the flower buds hanging limp, attached to the stem by a wisp of unchewed fiber.

Both earwigs and cutworms can be controlled by Bt, *Bacillus thuringiensis*, which bacterium interferes with their digestion, starving the beasts. Spinosad, an insecticide derived from another bacterium, is often added to organic slug baits; it causes hyperexcitation of the nervous system of the earwigs and cutworms upon ingestion, leading to prostration, paralysis, and eventual death. Because this is a pelleted product and placed on the ground, bees are not affected.

As for mammals, clematis are not deer-proof, but they are deer-resistant. There are lots of edibles deer like better.

Deer have kindly avoided both rhododendron and *Clematis patens*.

Propagation

The three main ways clematis are propagated are by semi-hardwood cuttings, seeds, and divisions. Briefly, cuttings require not only that the plant be at the right stage of growth but also rooting hormone, bottom heat, bottom watering, and lots of space for the flats of cuttings. So, for home gardeners, starting clematis from seed and making divisions are the easiest methods of propagation.

Well-rooted, happy cuttings of *Clematis* 'Brewster' (Montana Group).

Cleaning clematis seed amounts to removing the seed tail.

STARTING FROM SEED

Seeds are the simplest method of propagation. Cleaning clematis seed involves nothing more than removing the seed tail. Then, all you need is a quart zip-lock bag, two cups of perlite, and a half cup of water. Assume you can start 25 seeds per bag. Label the bag with the type of seed, the date it was started, and how many seeds are in it. Place the bag in a warm place where the sun won't shine on the plastic, thus cooking the seeds; artificial light doesn't matter. Please note that if you are starting the seeds of hybrids, you will get a wild mix of seedlings rarely bearing much resemblance to the parent plant. For starting clematis species, the baggie-plus-moist-perlite method works great.

Large seeds, such as those of the Viorna Group species, will germinate more quickly if they are soaked in room-temperature water for five days and the pericarp (outer seed coat) is removed.

Most clematis seed are too small to need this treatment. If the species comes from a cold climate (*Clematis alpina*, *C. koreana*, *C. patens*), cold stratification may be necessary to break dormancy, but this can be done by throwing the bag of seed into your refrigerator for four weeks. Write the date you started the cold stratification on the baggie. After four weeks, leave the seed at room temperature for four weeks, and then put the seed back into the cold for an additional four weeks. Often the seeds will begin to germinate in their second cold spell.

Some clematis, such as most of the species in the Tangutica/Orientalis Group, germinate quickly, in just two weeks. They are too tiny to be soaked and do not need cold.

Check the bags weekly to look for germinated seed. Once the first root (known as the radical) is an inch long, the infant should be removed from the bag and potted, even if the leaves have not emerged yet.

Count down the number of seedlings you have taken out of the baggie. Label the infant, cover it with a 0.25-inch (0.5-cm) layer of chicken grit or other fine gravel, and place the pot in a saucer where it can be watered from the bottom to avoid damping off.

As soon as the toddlers have roots at the drainage holes, move to the next-size pot, and finally finish the youngster in a 1-gallon pot.

Soaking and then removing the pericarp (outer seed coat) speeds germination for the Viorna Group species. Shown here, seed with pericarp half removed.

Two clear divisions and nice new shoots.

DIVIDING CLEMATIS

Splitting clematis crowns gives you nearly instant new plants! Have plenty of pots and soil ready, so the divisions don't lie around drying out. Taking divisions from clematis in containers is easiest, but digging up a vigorous clematis from the garden is only a bit heavier work.

When you see a clematis with several shoots coming from the ground, it is possible more than one crown has formed. Dig or unpot the root ball, wash the soil off, and see what you've got. When it is clear where new shoots are, detangle the roots—chopsticks are amazingly helpful for this part of the process.

How many divisions you get from a crown will depend upon what the plant presents to you, and how aggressive you are at making separations. Clematis are resilient, and with a little transplant tonic, will bounce back quickly. Plant the divisions into the size of pot you think will accommodate the remaining root system without being too large. If you are dividing a plant that was in the ground, the biggest remaining chunk should be replanted immediately.

Unbraiding the dreadlocks requires patience. Chopsticks are ideal tools for this.

A bounty of divisions!

WHERE TO BUY

AUSTRALIA

Alameda Homestead Nursery
112–116 Homestead Road
Berwick
Victoria 3806
ahn.com.au

BELGIUM

Böttcher Clematiskwekerij
Catherine Böttcher
Grote Leiestraat 141
(Nursery-Reinstraat)
8570 Anzegem
clematis-bottcher.be

CANADA

**Clearview Horticultural
Products Garden Shop**
27343 48th Avenue
Langley, British Columbia V2Z 2S8
homeofclematis.com

Gardens North
Box 370
Annapolis Royal, Nova Scotia B0S 1A0
gardensnorth.com

Humber Nurseries, Ltd.
8386 Highway 50
Brampton, Ontario L6T 0A5
gardencentre.com

FINLAND

Puutarhakeskus Sofianlehto
Sofianlehdonkatu 12
00610 Helsinki
sofianlehto.com

GERMANY

Baumschule Sachs
Grobstrückenweg 10
01445 Radebeul Cl. Gärtnerei
baumschule-sachs.de

Baumschule W. Kruse
Wallenbrücker Str. 14
49328 Melle-Westhoyel
clematis.de

Clematisspezialitäten Herian
Adelsweg 11
89440 Unterliezheim
clematis-herian.de

F M Westphal
Clematiskulturen
Peiner Hof 7/Peiner Haag 45
25497 Prisdorf
clematis-westphal.de

Münster Baumschulen
Bullendorf 19–20
25335 Altenmoor
clematis-muenster.de

ITALY

**Vivaio Le Clematis
di Daniela di Stefano**
Via Fresine Vasciotte, 38
03013 Ferentino (FR)
vivaioleclematis.com

JAPAN

Kasugai Garden Center
1709-120 Kakino
Tsurusato-cho
Toki-city
Gifu, 509-5312
clematis-net.com

LITHUANIA

Saulius Rimkevicius
Vysniu 7c
Siauliai 5412
angelfire.com/in/ClemLit/index.html

NEW ZEALAND

New Zealand Clematis Nurseries
67 Ngaio Street
St. Martins
Christchurch 2

Yaku Nursery
278 Tikorangi Road East
RD43, Waitara 4656
Taranaki
mrclematis.co.nz

UNITED KINGDOM

Clematis Choice
Lower Toollands
West Bagborough
Taunton
Somerset TA4 3EP
England
clematischoice.co.uk

Hawthorne Nursery
Marsh Road
Hesketh Bank nr. Preston
Lancastershire PR4 6XT
England
hawthornes-nursery.co.uk

Kevock Garden Plants
16 Kevock Road
Lasswade
Midlothian EH18 1HT
Scotland
kevockgarden.co.uk

Pennells Garden Centres
Newark Road South
Hykeham
Lincolnshire LN6 9NT
England
pennellsonline.co.uk

Pioneer Plant Nursery
Baldock Lane
Willian
Hertfordshire SG6 2AE
England
pioneerplantnursery.co.uk

Thorncroft Clematis
The Lings, Reymerston
Norwich
Norfolk NR9 4QG
England
thorncroftclematis.co.uk

Don Long
706-208-0678

UNITED STATES

Brushwood Nursery
706-548-1710
431 Hale Lane
Athens, Georgia 30607
gardenvines.com

Completely Clematis Nursery
217 Argilla Road
Ipswich, Massachusetts 01938
clematisnursery.com

Donahue's Clematis Specialists
420 SW 10th Street
Box 366
Faribault, Minnesota 55021
donahuesclematis.com

Far Reaches Farm
1818 Hastings Avenue
Port Townsend, Washington 98368
farreachesfarm.com

Joy Creek Nursery
20300 NW Watson Road
Scappoose, Oregon 97056
joycreek.com

Laporte Avenue Nursery
1950 Laporte Avenue
Fort Collins, Colorado 80521
laporteavenuenursery.com

Plant Delights Nursery
9241 Sauls Road
Raleigh, North Carolina 27603
plantdelights.com

Silver Star Vinery
31805 NE Clearwater Drive
Yacolt, Washington 98675
silverstarvinery.com

Spring Hill Nursery
110 W. Elm Street
Tipp City, Ohio 45371
springhillnursery.com

WHERE TO SEE

AUSTRALIA

Carole's Garden Clematis Nursery
94 Bungower Road
Somerville, Victoria 3912
National Collection Holder.

CANADA

UBC Botanical Garden
6804 SW Marine Drive
Vancouver, British Columbia V6T 1Z4
botanicalgarden.ubc.ca

FRANCE

Mairie de Paris
Direction des Parcs, Jardins & Espaces
Verts
1, Av. Gordon Bennett
75016 Paris
National Collection Holder.

JAPAN

Clematis-no-Oka
347-1 Clematis-no-Oka (Surugadaira)
Nagaizumi-cho
Shizuoka 411-0931
www.clematis-no-oka.co.jp

UNITED KINGDOM

Clematis Corner
15 Plough Close
Shillingford
Oxfordshire OX10 7EX
England
*National Collection of Herbaceous
Perennial Clematis.*

East Ruston Old Vicarage
East Ruston
Norwich
Norfolk NR12 9HN
England
e-ruston-oldvicaragegardens.co.uk

Floyd's Climbers and Clematis
At Showell Nurseries
Showell, Chippenham
Wiltshire SN15 2NU
England
floydsclimbers.co.uk
National Collection of Clematis koreana.

Great Dixter
Northiam, Rye
East Sussex TN31 6PH
England
greatdixter.co.uk

Hawthornes Nursery
Marsh Road
Hesketh Bank nr. Preston
Lancastershire PR4 6XT
England
hawthornes-nursery.co.uk
National Collection of Clematis viticella.

Longstock Park Nursery
Longstock, Stockbridge
Hampshire SO20 6EH
England
www.longstocknursery.co.uk
National Collection of Clematis viticella.

Roseland House
Charlie Pridham
Chacewater, Truro
Cornwall TR4 8QB
England
roselandhouse.co.uk
National Collection of Clematis viticella.

Rosewood
Keith Treadaway
Redberth nr. Tenby
Pembrokeshire SA70 8SA
Wales
National Collection of Clematis viorna.

Royal Horticulture Society Garden, Wisley
Woking
Surrey GU23 6QB
England
rhs.org.uk/gardens/wisley

Sissinghurst Castle Garden
Biddenden Road nr. Cranbrook
Kent TN17 2AB
England
nationaltrust.org.uk/
sissinghurst-castle-garden

Sunbury Walled Garden
Sunbury Park
Thames Street
Sunbury-on-Thames TW16 6AB
England
British Clematis Society Display Garden.

Treasures of Tenbury Ltd.
Burford House Gardens
Tenbury Wells
Worcestershire WR15 8HQ
England
*National Collection of Clematis texensis,
C. viticella, and others.*

Valerie Le May Neville-Parry
By the Way, Lodge Drove
Woodfalls
Salisbury SP5 2NH
England
clematismontana.co.uk
National Collection of Clematis montana.

UNITED STATES

Arnold Arboretum of Harvard University
M. Victor and Frances Leventritt Shrub
and Vine Garden
125 Arbor Way
Boston, Massachusetts 02130
arboretum.harvard.edu

Chicago Botanic Garden
1000 Cook Road
Glencoe, Illinois 60022
chicagobotanic.org

Denver Botanic Gardens
1007 York Street
Denver, Colorado 80206
botanicgardens.org

Joy Creek Nursery
20300 NW Watson Road
Scappoose, Oregon 97056
joycreek.com

Longwood Gardens
1001 Longwood Road
Kennett Square, Pennsylvania 19348
longwoodgardens.org

Rogerson Clematis Garden
Luscher Farm
125 Rosemont Road
West Linn, Oregon 97068
rogersonclematiscollection.org
Provisional Member,
North American Plant Collections
Consortium.

Scott Arboretum
Swarthmore College
500 College Avenue
Swarthmore, Pennsylvania 10081
scottarboretum.org

The Climbery
201 Buckwheat Bridge Road
Livingston, New York 12541
Private garden open regularly to the public.

FOR MORE INFORMATION

BOOKS

Beutler, Linda. 2004. *Gardening with Clematis*. Portland, Oregon: Timber Press.

Evison, Raymond. 2007. *Clematis for Small Spaces*. Portland, Oregon: Timber Press.

Fretwell, Barry. 1989. *Clematis*. Deer Park, Wisconsin: Capability's Books.

Gooch, Ruth, and Jonathan Gooch. 2011. *Clematis: The Essential Guide*. Marlborough, Wiltshire: The Crowood Press.

Grey-Wilson, Christopher. 2000. *Clematis the Genus*. Portland, Oregon: Timber Press.

Johnson, Magnus. 2001. *The Genus Clematis*. Södertälje: Magnus Johnsons Plantskola AB.

Royal Horticultural Society. 2002. *The International Clematis Register and Checklist*. Compiled by Victoria Matthews. London: Royal Horticultural Society.

Royal Horticultural Society. 2006. *The International Clematis Register and Checklist, Second Supplement*. Compiled by Victoria Matthews. London: Royal Horticultural Society.

Royal Horticultural Society. 2009. *The International Clematis Register and Checklist, Third Supplement*. Compiled by Duncan Donald. London: Royal Horticultural Society.

Royal Horticultural Society. 2012. *The International Clematis Register and Checklist, Fourth Supplement*. Compiled by Duncan Donald. London: Royal Horticultural Society.

Toomey, Mary K., and Everett Leeds. 2001. *An Illustrated Encyclopedia of Clematis*. Portland, Oregon: Timber Press.

WEBSITES

Clematis in Seattle:
clematisinseattle.com

Clematis from Seed:
bcollingwood.com/index1.htm

Clematis on the Web:
clematis.hull.ac.uk/index.cfm

Rogerson Clematis Garden:
rogersonclematiscollection.org

Ton Hannink: members.home.nl/
hanninkj/eigenclm.htm#B

ORGANIZATIONS

British Clematis Society:
britishclematis.org.uk

Estonian Clematis Society:
hot.ee/clematis1/index.html

**Friends of the Rogerson
Clematis Collection:**
rogersonclematiscollection.org

International Clematis Society:
clematisinternational.com

HARDINESS ZONE TEMPERATURES

USDA ZONES & CORRESPONDING TEMPERATURES

Temp °F			Zone	Temp °C		
-60	to	-55	1a	-51	to	-48
-55	to	-50	1b	-48	to	-46
-50	to	-45	2a	-46	to	-43
-45	to	-40	2b	-43	to	-40
-40	to	-35	3a	-40	to	-37
-35	to	-30	3b	-37	to	-34
-30	to	-25	4a	-34	to	-32
-25	to	-20	4b	-32	to	-29
-20	to	-15	5a	-29	to	-26
-15	to	-10	5b	-26	to	-23
-10	to	-5	6a	-23	to	-21
-5	to	0	6b	-21	to	-18
0	to	5	7a	-18	to	-15
5	to	10	7b	-15	to	-12
10	to	15	8a	-12	to	-9
15	to	20	8b	-9	to	-7
20	to	25	9a	-7	to	-4
25	to	30	9b	-4	to	-1
30	to	35	10a	-1	to	2
35	to	40	10b	2	to	4
40	to	45	11a	4	to	7
45	to	50	11b	7	to	10
50	to	55	12a	10	to	13
55	to	60	12b	13	to	16
60	to	65	13a	16	to	18
65	to	70	13b	18	to	21

FIND HARDINESS MAPS ON THE INTERNET.

United States usna.usda.gov/Hardzone/ushzmap.html
Canada planthardiness.gc.ca
Europe houzz.com/europeZoneFinder

ACKNOWLEDGMENTS

For Brewster, with immortal gratitude.

Fiction or nonfiction, writing a book is a journey. Tom Fischer, senior acquisitions editor for Timber Press, was the person who invited me to make this one. The clematis community is close-knit, and I take a risk by singling out just a few folks from the many who are great friends and people of influence, but I shall. Thanks to Sue Austin (thanks for the Holy Grail), Bruce Bailey, Diana Breen, Lyndy Broder, Mike Brown, Cole Burrell (thanks for the avian Holy Grail), Mikiyoshi and Tomoko Chikuma, James Earl, Debbie Fischer, Maurice Horn, Maureen Hudson, Jeff Jabco, Panayoti Kelaidis, Klaus Körber, Everett and Carol Leeds, Dan Long, Barbara and Szczepan Marczynski, Roy and Angela Nunn, Werner Stastny, Kozo and Mikiko Sugimoto, Karin Sundström, Mary Toomey, Penny Vogel, Sixten and Ingar Widberg, Fiona and Ken Woolfenden.

All the above, and clematarians everywhere, owe a huge debt of gratitude to our International Clematis Registrars, Victoria Matthews (retired) and Duncan Donald (wishes he were retired, no doubt). That they are delightful people is the icing on the cake.

If you look carefully here, you will see names from all over. Join the International Clematis Society and see the world, I kid you not! That journey thing I said before is really true.

Locally, I am enhanced in every way by the Friends of the Rogerson Clematis Collection. Their faith in me is a constant source of inspiration to work harder and learn more.

And now, for all the nurseries and gardeners whose plants and works of the heart are pictured, you have provided the beauty contained here. Some names are repeated from the above list, but good things bear repeating: Lyndy Broder, Stockbridge, Georgia; Brushwood Nursery, Athens, Georgia; Betty Crisp, Rockaway Beach, Oregon; James Earl, Spokane, Washington; Erlabrunn, Germany (yep, the whole village); Sally Geist, Portland, Oregon; Joy Creek Nursery, Scappoose, Oregon; Kinzy Faire, Estacada, Oregon; Lucy and Fred Hardiman, Portland, Oregon; Phyllis Hathaway, Spokane, Washington; Longwood Gardens, Kennett Square, Pennsylvania; Roger Lorenzen, Tukwila, Washington; Barbara and Szczepan Marczynski, Warszawska, Poland; Ernie and Marietta O'Byrne, Eugene, Oregon; Jan Robertson, Portland, Oregon; Rogerson Clematis Garden/Friends of the Rogerson Clematis Collection, West Linn, Oregon; Silver Star Vinery, Yacolt, Washington; Mike Snyder, Beaverton, Oregon. If I have forgotten anyone or any place, I am sincerely sorry.

And on the home front, thanks to Larry Beutler, Tess Waterdog Trueheart, Jacqueline Mitzel, Dorothy and David Rodal (who could be in all three lists), Mike Snyder, Betty Crisp, and all the friends and family who keep me going when I take on a project like this.

PHOTO CREDITS

COVER: Heather Edwards/GAP.

RICHARD BLOOM/GAP, page 158 (right).

FRIENDS OF THE ROGERSON CLEMATIS COLLECTION, by Brewster Rogerson and the author, pages 67 (left), 71 (left), 74, 75, 94 (right), 116, 138 (bottom), 147, 197, 204 (left).

MAURICE HORN, pages 133 (left), 164 (right), 183 (left).

BOB HYLAND, page 145 (left).

PANAYOTI KELAIDIS, page 182 (right).

DAN LONG, Brushwood Nursery, pages 71 (right), 85, 92 (left), 97 (right), 119 (right), 124 (right), 130, 166, 183 (right).

SZCZEPAN MARCZYNSKI, page 95.

SARAH MILHOLLIN, pages 2–3, 4–5, 7, 10–11, 13 (top), 38–39, 46, 62–63, 172 (left), 210–211, 214, 232.

SUE MILLIKEN, Far Reaches Farm, page 194 (left).

HOWARD RICE/GAP, page 162 (left).

SABINA RUBER/GAP, page 184 (left).

All other photos are by the author.

INDEX

Abelia ×*grandiflora*, 91, 170
Acer circinatum, 183
Acer palmatum, 103
   'Fjellheim', 21
acidic soil, 141
acid-loving shrubs, 23
alcohol, 36
alfalfa pellets, 18
alstroemeria, 131
Arctostaphylos uva-ursi 'Massachusetts', 14
army worm, 232
Asai, Sano, 85
Asia, 40

Bacillus thuringiensis (Bt), 232
Balearic Islands, 9
Baltensparger, Urs, 201
barberries, 20
Barron, Will, 138
Bees' Nursery, 71
"Beijing patens," 44
bell-shaped flowers, 48, 49
berberis, 136
Berberis darwinii 'Nana', 173
bird's nest spruce, 169
black spot, 18
Blooms of Bressingham, 207
bloom time, 17, 42, 46, 58
blue passionflower, 171
bone meal, 213
bonnet-shaped flowers, 48, 49
box elder, 144
Brooklyn Botanic Garden, 133

California lilac, 209
Callery pear, 73
camellias, 23, 78, 129
Canada, 129, 138
Ceanothus, 209
Cedrus deodara 'Snow Sprite', 24
Chalk Hill Clematis, 35
Chamaecyparis, 24

Chamaecyparis lawsoniana
   'Blue Surprise', 86
Chatto, Beth, 187
Chickamauga Battlefield site, 175
chicken wire, 23, 130
China, 45–46, 49, 56, 148, 174, 175, 191, 194, 202
Chinese witch hazel, 70
Cistus, 204, 206
"clear cut" method, 55
Clearview Horticultural Products, 129, 138
Clematis, 15
   'Abundance', 12, 140
   Alaina 'Evipo056', 64, 199
   'Alba Luxurians', 142
   'Albina Plena', 20
   'Alionushka', 194
   'Allanah', 65, 93
   'Andromeda', 66
   'Anita', 144, 177
   'Apple Blossom', 145
   'Arabella', 14, 145, 184, 186, 191
   Arctic Queen 'Evitwo', 67
   'Asao', 67
   Avant-Garde 'Evipo033', 148
   'Barbara Dibley', 68
   'Barbara Jackman', 69, 76
   'Beauty of Worcester', 103
   'Bees' Jubilee', 71
   'Bells of Emei Shan', 148, 194
   'Betty Corning', 139, 149
   Bijou 'Evipo030', 71
   'Bill MacKenzie', 33, 139, 150, 171, 176, 217
   'Blekitny Aniol' Blue Angel, 151
   'Blue Belle', 152
   'Bluebird', 82, 153
   'Blue Dancer', 153, 165

   'Blue Eyes', 72
   'Blue Ravine', 55, 73
   Bonanza 'Evipo031', 154
   'Brewster', 233
   'Broughton Star', 155
   'Brunette', 156
   'Buckland Beauty', 225
   'Burma Star', 85
   'Candida', 75, 194
   'Candy Stripe', 76
   'Carmencita', 158
   'Cecile', 159, 163
   'Chalcedony', 103
   'Chatsworth', 227
   'Clochette Pride', 162
   'Comtesse de Bouchaud', 77, 199
   'Constance', 163
   'Countess of Lovelace', 23
   'Crimson King', 78
   'Daniel Deronda', 79, 87
   'Danuta', 80
   'Dark Dancer', 165
   'Dark Eyes', 165
   'Doctor Ruppel', 80
   'Duchess of Albany', 34, 167, 199
   'Duchess of Edinburgh', 81
   'Early Sensation', 169
   'Edomurasaki' Blue Bird, 82
   'Emilia Plater', 169
   'Ernest Markham', 83, 123
   'Étoile Rose', 35, 40, 170
   'Étoile Violette', 32, 35, 150, 171
   'Fair Rosamond', 84
   'Fairy Blue' Crystal Fountain, 84
   'Fireworks', 113
   Fleuri 'Evipo042', 19, 85
   'Fond Memories', 86, 115
   'Frau Mikiko', 87
   'Freda', 57
   'Fujimusume', 87, 104

Clematis [*continued*]
Gazelle 'Evipo014', 182
'General Sikorski', 87, 88, 104
'Gillian Blades', 89
'Gipsy Queen', 19, 44, 46, 103
'Golden Harvest', 176
Golden Tiara 'Kugotia', 229
'Gravetye Beauty', 19, 94, 176, 204
'Guernsey Cream', 55, 90
'Hagley Hybrid' Pink Chiffon, 91
'Hakuokan', 13, 91
'Halina Noll', 24
'Hayate', 92
'Hebe's Lip', 109
'Helios', 177
'Helsingborg', 177
'Henryi', 92, 128, 221
'H. F. Young', 84
'Honora', 93
'Hoshi-no-flamenco', 94
'Huldine', 180
'Huvi', 222
'Innocent Glance', 95
Inspiration 'Zoin', 181
'Iubileinyi-70', 18, 96
'Jackmanii', 46, 97, 103, 139, 171, 225
Jackmanii Purpurea 'Zojapur', 97
'Jan Lindmark', 163
'Jan Pawel II', 98
'Jenny', 28, 183, 214
'Jenny Keay', 183
John Howells 'Zojohnhowells', 184
'John Paul II', 98
'Jubilee-70', 96
'Julileinyi-70', 96
'Julka', 19, 99
'Juuli', 184
'Kacper', 99, 105
'Kardynal Wyszynski', 99
'Kermesina', 148
'King Edward VII', 101
Kingfisher 'Evipo037', 21, 101

'King George V', 102
'Kiri Te Kanawa', 103
'Lady Betty Balfour', 103
'Lady Northcliffe', 104
'Leda', 109
'Lincoln Star', 113
'Little Artist', 28, 29
'Lord Herschell', 186
'Louise Rowe', 7, 106, 110
'Lunar Lass', 186
'Madame Baron-Veillard', 107, 109
'Madame Julia Correvon', 32, 187
'Maksymilian Kolbe', 20
'Marcelina', 108
'Margaret Hunt', 109
'Margaret Jones', 119
'Markham's Pink', 189
'Maureen', 109
'Mikelite', 22
'Minuet', 190
'Miranda', 27, 186, 191
'Monte Cassino', 125
'Mrs. George Jackman', 110
'Mrs. N. Thompson', 99, 111, 137
'Mrs. Robert Brydon', 192
'Mrs. Spencer Castle', 111
'My Angel', 53
'Negritianka', 42, 112
'Nelly Moser', 71, 111, 113
'Niobe', 25, 114, 125
'Odoriba', 193
'Omoshiro', 46, 115
'Pamela Jackman', 143
'Pamiat Serdsta', 42, 194
'Perle d'Azur', 26, 115, 131, 199
'Perrin's Pride', 116, 218
Petit Faucon 'Evisix', 196
'Peveril Pearl', 55, 117
'Piilu' Little Duckling, 118, 224
'Pinky', 119
'Polish Spirit', 26, 198
'Prince Charles', 34, 199
'Princess Diana', 139, 200, 228
Princess Kate 'Zoprika', 200

'Purpurea Plena Elegans', 201
Rebecca 'Evipo016', 119
Reflections 'Evipo035', 120
'Rhapsody', 120
'Roguchi', 202, 231
'Roko-Kolla', 121
'Romantika', 230
Rosemoor 'Evipo002', 121
'Rouge Cardinal', 122, 133
'Royal Velours', 13, 203
'Rubra Grandiflora', 187
'Ruby', 163, 204
'Rüütel', 123
'Sano-no-murasaki', 85
'Semu', 30, 124, 219
'Sir Trevor Lawrence', 101, 167, 204
'Sizaia Ptitsa', 205
'Snow Queen', 124
'Solidarnosc', 35, 125
'Solina', 35
'Stasik', 229
'Tenri no Asagasumi', 126
'Teshio', 127
'Toki', 55, 128
'Tsuzuki', 128
'Utopia', 115
Vancouver 'Morning Mist', 129, 223
'Venosa Violacea', 8, 9, 190, 208
'Veronica's Choice', 130
'Victoria', 131
'Ville de Lyon', 74, 132, 187
'Viola', 16, 119, 226, 230
'Violet Elizabeth', 111
'Voluceau', 133
'Vyvyan Pennell', 110, 130, 133
'Warszawska Nike' Midnight Showers, 135, 181
'Warszawska Olga', 136
'Warwickshire Rose', 208
'W. E. Gladstone', 136
'Westerplatte', 125
'White Swan', 209
'Wildfire', 137
'Will Barron', 138
'Will Goodwin', 87, 138, 139
Wisley 'Evipo001', 139, 217

Clematis addisonii, 141
Clematis afoliata, 9
Clematis alpina, 59–60, 234
   'Pamela Jackman', 7, 60, 143
   'Stolwijk Gold', 143
Clematis armandii
   'Apple Blossom', 58
   'Snowdrift', 58, 146
Clematis ×*aromatica*, 147
Clematis Atragene Group, 31,
   59–61, 82, 156, 162, 177,
   204, 209
Clematis baldwinii, 55
Clematis carrizoensis, 9
Clematis ×*cartmanii*, 158
   'Joe', 169
Clematis chiisanensis 'Lemon
   Bells', 160
Clematis chrysocoma, 57
Clematis cirrhosa
   var. *balearica*, 161
   'Ourika Valley', 24, 161
   var. *purpurascens* 'Freck-
   les', 24, 162
Clematis Cirrhosa Group, 161–
   162, 221
Clematis crispa, 9, 117, 164, 193
Clematis ×*diversifolia*
   'Eriostemon', 43
   'Heather Herschell', 33,
   166, 186
Clematis ×*durandii*, 168, 191,
   205
Clematis Evergreen Group, 31,
   33, 58, 145, 158, 169, 186,
   215, 220–221
Clematis fasciculiflora, 172
Clematis flammula, 172, 205
Clematis Flammula Group,
   147, 201
Clematis florida, 44–46, 86,
   115, 208, 216
   var. *flore-pleno* 'Plena', 45,
   46, 47
   var. *florida* 'Sieboldiana',
   46, 47
   var. *plena*, 45
Clematis fremontii, 173
Clematis fruticosa 'Mongolian
   Gold', 174

Clematis fusca, 49, 175
Clematis glaucophylla, 9, 175
Clematis gracilifolia, 56
Clematis heracleifolia 'Cassan-
   dra', 178
Clematis Heracleifolia Group,
   178, 192, 207, 213
Clematis hirsutissima, 179
Clematis hirsutissima var. *scot-
   tii*, 33, 170
Clematis ianthina, 49, 175
Clematis integrifolia, 6, 40–43,
   147, 166, 168, 174, 181, 202
   'Alba', 182
   Mongolian Bells 'PSHar-
   lan', 182
   'Pangbourne Pink', 166, 195
   'Rosea', 166, 181
Clematis Integrifolia Group,
   28, 42, 43, 186, 194, 202,
   222
Clematis intricata, 53
Clematis japonica, 183
   var. *obvallata*, 183
Clematis koreana, 59, 160, 234
   var. *fragrans*, 185
   var. *lutea*, 160
Clematis lanuginosa, 46, 75,
   168
Clematis macropetala, 59
Clematis mandshurica, 55, 188
Clematis marata, 186
Clematis marmoraria, 6, 158
Clematis montana, 183
   'Marjorie', 155
   var. *rubens*, 56, 57
   'White Fragrance', 191
   aff. *wilsonii* DJHC796, 56
   var. *wilsonii*, 57
   var. *wilsonii* hort., 9, 56, 191,
   228
Clematis Montana Group, 28,
   32, 56–57, 119, 155, 172, 183,
   191, 208, 219, 220–221
Clematis occidentalis, 60
   var. *grosseserrata*, 59
Clematis ochotensis, 59, 177
Clematis orientalis, 54, 177
Clematis otophora, 194
Clematis paniculata, 158, 205

Clematis patens, 44–46, 55, 75,
   94, 121, 128, 230, 234
   'John Gould Veitch', 45
   'Manshuu Ki', 94
   'Standishii', 45
   'Yukiokoshi', 44
Clematis pitcheri, 197
Clematis recta
   'Midnight Masquerade',
   201
   'Purpurea', 201
Clematis rehderiana, 202
Clematis repens, 148
Clematis reticulata, 50, 202
Clematis sibirica, 59, 209
Clematis spooneri, 56
Clematis tangutica, 54
Clematis Tangutica/Orientalis
   Group, 54–55, 139, 144,150,
   171, 176, 177, 216, 234
Clematis terniflora, 172, 188,
   205
Clematis texensis, 9, 40, 49–52,
   132, 170, 175, 176, 187, 193,
   199, 206
Clematis Texensis Group, 26,
   50–53, 61, 167, 200, 208,
   213–214, 216, 222
Clematis tibetana, 54
Clematis tubulosa, 178
   Alan Bloom 'Alblo', 207
Clematis urticifolia, 6
Clematis vinacea, 53
Clematis viorna, 48
Clematis Viorna Group, 49–53,
   175, 222, 225, 234
Clematis vitalba, 9
Clematis viticella, 40–43, 46,
   55, 147, 149, 166, 170, 187,
   208, 216
   'Flore Pleno', 40, 201
Clematis Viticella Group, 32,
   40, 116, 154, 158, 165, 170,
   180, 184, 199, 216, 225
climbing roses, 17–18
   with large-flowered
   hybrids, 73, 90, 91, 115, 132
   with small-flowered clematis, 151, 167, 180, 200
color, 19, 23

combinations, 12
    clematis and roses, 16–19
    clematis with clematis,
        32–33, 142, 150, 152
    color and texture contrast
        in, 33
    with large-flowered
        hybrids, 67, 93, 95, 109, 111,
        119, 126–127
    with small-flowered clema-
        tis, 135, 158
conifers, 24, 68, 76, 106, 129,
    144, 169, 194
containers, 28–31, 74
coreopsis, 178
cornels, 201
Cornus controversa 'Variegata',
    13, 144, 203
Cornus florida, 201
Cornus mas 'Variegata', 127
Cotinus coggygria
    Golden Spirit 'Ancot', 168
    'Royal Purple', 22, 70
Cotinus 'Grace', 70
cotoneaster, 101
cowslip-scented clematis, 202
Cranford Rose Garden, 133
Cryptomeria japonica
    'Black Dragon', 194
    'Elegans', 24
cultivation, 42, 45–46, 49, 54
cut flowers, 35–37, 193
cutting garden, 188
cutworm, 232

dahlia, 27
Dahlia 'Giraffe', 167
daphnes, 120, 173
daylilies, 131, 178
deadheading, 55, 227
decorative use, 40, 107, 139
deer, 232
Denver Botanic Gardens, 174,
    179, 182
designing, 12–37
deutzia, 18
Deutzia ×*hybrida* 'Magicien', 83
Deutzia setchuenensis var. *cor-*
    ymbiflora, 185

diseases, 18–19, 230–231
dividing, 235
dolomite lime, 141
Douglas fir, 171
drought tolerant, 26, 42

earwigs, 232
Edelweiss Nursery, 201
Edwards, Allanah, 65
elderberry, 70
England, 9, 45, 61, 114, 124,
    203, 230
Epimedium pinnatum subsp.
    colchicum, 187
Estonia, 184, 230
ethyl alcohol, 36
Euonymus, 166
Euonymus fortunei 'Emerald
    Gaiety', 92, 171
Europe, 40, 45, 78, 125, 135, 147,
    181, 194
Everclear, 36
evergreen clematis, 58, 172,
    219
evergreen hedges, 93, 143, 153,
    154, 177
Evison, Raymond, 74, 94, 98,
    119, 139, 148

Far Reaches Farm, 194
feeding, 18
fencing cloth, 23, 130, 140, 143,
    144, 176, 177, 187, 229
ferns, 148
fertilizing, 18, 28
Fischer, Debbie, 205
Fisk, Jim, 89
Fisk's Nursery, 114
floral preservative, 36
floribunda roses, 16, 17, 18
Florida, 55
forsythia, 166
fragrant blossoms, 9
France, 206
Franczak, Stefan, 80, 135, 136,
    169
Fretwell, Barry, 85, 186, 191
frikartii asters, 192
Frost, Pam, 187

fuchsias, 103, 193
Fuchsia 'Whiteknights Ame-
    thyst', 193
fungal diseases, 18
fungicides, 230

Gay, Jane, 181
George VI (king of England),
    102
George V (king of England),
    102
Georgia, 173, 175
Geranium Rozanne 'Gerwat',
    109, 147
geraniums, 147
golden chain tree, 138
golden hop, 187
gravel gardens, 141, 158, 174,
    179, 182, 186, 200, 206
Gravetye Manor, 152, 190, 203,
    204
groundcover
    large-flowered hybrids as,
        80, 87, 99, 117, 136, 137, 139
    small-flowered clematis
        as, 148, 167, 169, 176, 183,
        184, 186, 192, 194, 200,
        205–206

Hamamelis, 103, 163
Hamernik, Harlan, 182
hardiness zones, 28
Hayakawa, Hiroshi, 84
heleniums, 178, 207
Helianthus, 207
Helianthus ×*multiflorus* 'Ane-
    moniflorus Flore Pleno',
    25
hellstrips, 182
herbaceous perennials, 25–27,
    42, 132
hibiscus, 114
Hibiscus 'Robert Fleming', 25
Hill, Josephine, 98
Himalayan blackberry, 89
Hinkley, Dan, 56, 57, 148
Hinoki cypress, 24
hips, 17
hog wire, 214, 229

Hokkaido, 127
honeysuckles, 158
hops, 158
Horn, Maurice, 124
Hosta 'Osprey', 125
hostas, 117, 137
Howells, John, 184, 191
hummingbirds, 9, 172, 175,
    202, 206
Humulus lupulus 'Aureus', 187
hybrids, 9
hybrid tea roses, 18
hydrangea
    with large-flowered
        hybrids, 17, 20–21, 71, 76,
        87, 136
    with small-flowered clem-
        atis, 145, 156, 164, 166, 181,
        205
Hydrangea macrophylla
    'Glowing Embers', 122
    'Lemon Wave', 82
    'Nigra', 205
Hydrangea paniculata 'Lime-
    light', 30
Hypericum forrestii, 65
Hypericum ×*inodorum* 'Sum-
    mergold', 119
hypericums, 65
hypertufa, 33

Imperata cylindrica 'Rubra',
    176
insecticide, 232
International Clematis Soci-
    ety, 9, 108, 169, 175
Ipomoea, 190
Iris 'Penny Lane', 27

Jackman's Nursery, 49, 84,
    97, 167
Japan, 35, 44–46, 49, 61, 119,
    127, 175, 193
Japanese bloodgrass, 176
Japanese maple, 101, 103, 202
Japanese snowbell, 138
Johnson, Magnus, 59, 158, 182
Joy Creek Nursery, 124, 165,
    202

Juniperus communis 'Gold
    Cone', 24
juvenile wilt disease, 230

Kansas, 221
Keay, Alister, 93, 183, 199
Kendrick Lake Park, 174
Kinzy Faire, 203
Kivistik, Uno, 118, 121
Korea, 6, 49

Laburnum anagyroides, 138
large-flowered hybrids, 13,
    42, 142
    with conifers, 24
    in containers, 30–31
    as cut flowers, 35
    development of, 44–46
    with herbaceous perenni-
        als, 25–26
    in mixed borders, 20–23
    planting, 215
    pruning, 221–226
    with roses, 16, 18
    seedheads, 55
    selections for the garden,
        64–139
    siting, 217–219
    supporting structures for,
        229
leather flowers, 49
Lemoine et Fils, 49
Lijiang spruce, 57
lilacs, 107, 113, 125, 143, 177
lilies, 200
Lilium sargentiae, 200
Linnaeus, Carl, 59
liquors, 36
lists of clematis
    Award of Garden Merit, 15
    for beginners, 9, 169
    for bright exposures, 216
    for broad blossoms, 223
    for containers, 31
    for low-light exposures, 219
    smaller large-flowered
        hybrids, 224
    for troughs, 33
Lloyd, Christopher, 204

Loropetalum chinense var.
    rubrum, 70

magnesium, 28
magnolia, 115, 140
Magnolia ×*soulangeana*, 115
Magnolia stellata, 115
Mahar, Dulcy, 122
Marczynski, Szczepan, 95,
    115, 125
marguerite daisies, 118
Markham, Ernest, 152, 190,
    204
Mason, David, 150
methyl alcohol, 36
Michaelmas daisies, 25, 84, 178
Miscanthus sinensis
    'Gold Bar', 177
    'Gold Breeze', 177
mixed borders, 20–23, 87, 145,
    195
mock-orange, 18, 103, 137, 196
Monarda 'Violet Queen', 25
Mongolia, 174, 175, 182
moon garden, 172
Morel, Francisque, 49, 176,
    190, 203
morning glories, 190
moss, 148
Mount Emei Shan, 148

native range, 40
native species, 49
Netherlands, 35, 45
New Zealand, 6, 61, 93, 158,
    186, 199, 205
nitrogen–phosphorus–potas-
    sium (N–P–K) fertil-
    izer, 18
nodding virgin's bower, 202
Nordic Arboretum Commit-
    tee, 185
North America, 49–53
Nunn, Roy, 124

Oregon, 80, 122, 124, 165, 203,
    213
organic rose and flower food,
    213, 214

Orienpet lilies, 26
ornamental grasses, 177, 207
oyster shells, 141

Panicum virgatum 'Heavy
    Metal', 177
partial shade borders, 26
Passiflora caerulea, 171
penstemon, 131, 204
peonies, 132
pests, 232
Philadelphus, 18, 103, 196
    'Belle Étoile', 196
    'Innocence', 137
Phoma clematidina, 230
Picea abies 'Nidiformis', 169
Picea likiangensis, 57
planting, 23, 212–215
Plant Select program, 182
Poland, 61, 80, 95, 108, 114, 125,
    135, 136, 169
pollinator attractors, 9
powdery mildew, 18, 230–231
propagation, 233–235
pruning, 17, 44, 55, 58, 213, 215,
    220–225
purplebell vine, 190
Pyrus calleryana, 97
Pyrus salicifolia 'Pendula',
    111, 184

Rhodochiton atrosanguineus,
    190
rhododendron, 23, 71, 78, 80,
    113, 139, 143, 148, 177, 201
Rhododendron 'Cynthia', 67
Ribes sanguineum 'King
    Edward VII', 101
Robinson, William, 152, 176,
    190, 204
rock gardens, 169, 173, 200,
    204
rockroses, 204, 206
Rocky Mountains, 179
Rogerson, Brewster, 97, 111
Rogerson Clematis Collec-
    tion, 97
Rogerson Clematis Garden,
    46, 175, 213, 223

roots, 27
Rosa
    'Cerise Bouquet', 66
    'Darlow's Enigma', 96
    Double Delight 'Andeli', 74
    'Dusky Maiden', 19
    'Félicité Perpétue', 16
    'Great Western', 16
    'Hebe's Lip', 74
    Jayne Austin 'Ausbreak', 79,
    96
    'La Belle Sultane', 19
    'Leda', 74
    'Madame Isaac Pereire', 83
    Monkey Business 'Jacfrara',
    18
    'New Dawn', 180
    'Paul's Lemon Pillar', 82
    'Robin Hood', 66
    'Shropshire Lass', 82
    'Sombreuil', 208
    'Zéphirine Drouhin', 83
Rosa glauca, 111
Rosa ×odorata 'Mutabilis', 19,
    100
Rosa palustris, 175
Rosa rugosa, 103
Rosa sericea subsp. *pteracan-
    tha* f. *omeiensis*, 57
Rosen, Murray, 35
roses, 16–19
Royal Horticultural Society, 15,
    94, 139
rudbeckias, 207
Russia, 175
rust, 18

Salix integra 'Hakuro-nishiki',
    184
Sambucus nigra f. *porphyro-
    phylla* 'Eva' Black Lace,
    70, 96
Sanders, Chris, 97, 176
scarlet lady, 206
scarlet leather flower, 206
seedheads, 54, 55, 73, 90, 117,
    144, 164, 169, 175, 176
seeds, 234
selecting, 212–215

shrub roses
    with large-flowered
        hybrids, 79, 82, 83, 87, 103,
        117, 121, 127, 136
    with small-flowered clem-
        atis, 142, 144, 147, 166, 176,
        181, 194
shrubs
    combining clematis with,
        20–23, 73, 95, 120
    dark-foliaged, 70
    deciduous, 20, 87, 145, 161,
        174, 175
    dwarf, 78, 173
    evergreen, 20, 110, 120, 129
    gold-foliaged, 65
    gray-foliaged, 82, 111, 165
    large, 75, 76, 80–83, 111, 127,
        140, 149
    later-flowering, 96
    medium-sized, 105, 114, 133,
        137
    mixed borders, 87
    small, 72, 84–85, 91, 99,
        104–105, 121, 123–128
    variegated, 82, 99
Siberia, 6
Siebold, Philipp von, 45
Silver Star Vinery, 12, 205
silver weeping pear, 111, 184
Sissinghurst Castle, 115
siting, 216–219
Skeggs-Gooch, Peter, 230
Skinner, Frank, 153
slugs, 230, 232
small-flowered clematis, 31,
    35, 55, 139, 140–209
smokebush, 70
snails, 230
Snoeijer, Wim, 97
soil, 28
solanums, 158
South America, 80
South Korea, 160
Spinosad, 232
Spiraea japonica, 92
spirea, 20, 87
Styrax japonicus, 138
sugar bowls, 179

Sugimoto, Kozo, 87
Sugimoto, Mikiko, 87
sunflowers, 207
supporting structures, 32
    arbors, 93, 97, 98, 107, 112,
        133, 151, 160, 176
    arches, 108, 131, 165
    built structures, 92, 97
    for climbing roses, 17–18
    columns, 70, 84, 86, 90, 97,
        126, 140, 143, 144, 177, 187
    for evergreen clematis, 58
    fences, 77, 103, 127, 131, 133,
        148, 160, 177, 191, 200, 202
    gazebos, 107, 176
    obelisk, 77
    peony cage, 141, 145, 181,
        182, 186, 201
    pergolas, 93, 144
    porches, 97, 103
    posts, 126, 140, 143, 144, 176,
        177, 187, 214, 228–229
    providing, 228–229
    trellises, 65, 80, 81, 97, 103,
        106, 111, 120, 133, 154, 159,
        161–162, 177, 189, 193, 200,
        208
    tripod, 90
    tuteurs, 9, 70, 88, 121, 124,
        133
swamp hyacinth, 164
swamp rose, 175
Sweden, 182
sweet autumn clematis, 205
Symphyotrichum, 25
Symphyotrichum novi-belgii
    'Lady in Blue', 84
    'Little Carlow', 84
Syringa Tinkerbelle 'Bail-
    belle', 125
Syringa vulgaris 'Miss Ellen
    Willmott', 114

tall bearded iris, 191
Tennessee, 53
Texas, 9, 206
thatch, 58
Thorncroft Clematis, 230

Thujopsis dolabrata 'Nana',
    101, 169
tidying, 227
tomato fertilizer, 28
Toomey, Mary, 160
trees, 165
    deciduous, 140
    small, 21, 73, 115, 131, 138,
        140, 144, 149, 193, 201
    spring-flowering, 75, 97
trees, fruit, 140, 201
    dwarf, 151
    semi-dwarf, 140
troughs, 33, 158, 173, 179
Tsuga canadensis
    'Gentsch White', 165
    'Summer Snow', 165

Ukraine, 96
United States, 35, 36, 49, 78, 92,
    116, 164, 179, 205–206
University of Georgia, 108
urn-shaped flowers, 48, 49

viburnum, 92, 102, 135, 153, 163
Viburnum opulus
    'Compactum', 135
    'Roseum', 127
Viburnum plicatum f.
    tomentosum
    'Mariesii', 153
    'Molly Schroeder', 20
Viburnum tinus, 204
Viburnum tinus 'Bewley's Var-
    iegated', 82
vine maple, 183
Virginia, 141
virgin's bower, 40
Vitex agnus-castus, 96
Vitis vinifera 'Purpurea', 133

Washington, 194
Waterperry Gardens, 150
Weigela
    'Bristol Ruby', 137
    'Florida Variegata', 168
weigelas, 137, 145
wild populations, 45

Wilson, E. H. ("Chinese"), 45,
    56–57, 191
wilt, 230
wisteria, 116
witch hazel, 103, 163
Wokingensis hybrids, 167

yews, 65, 110

ABOUT THE AUTHOR

LINDA BEUTLER's first love in her own garden was growing flowers and foliage for cutting. That focus changed when Linda purchased her first clematis as a misnamed plant. This passion for clematis led to the publication of her first book, *Gardening with Clematis* (Timber Press, 2004).

Linda has been the curator of the Rogerson Clematis Collection since 2007, and in 2013, she was elected the first woman and first American president of the International Clematis Society. She is an active member of the Hardy Plant Society of Oregon and many other garden and plant societies. She lectures nationally on numerous gardening topics and is a garden writer for both local and national publications, including *Organic Gardening*, *Pacific Horticulture*, and *Portrait of Portland*.

LOMA SMITH

Front cover: *Clematis* 'Perle d'Azur'
Spine: *Clematis* 'Fond Memories'
Title page: *Clematis* 'Pinky'
Contents page: *Clematis montana* aff. *wilsonii*

The Haseltine Building
133 S.W. Second Avenue, Suite 450
Portland, Oregon 97204-3527

For details on other Timber Press books and to
sign up for our newsletters, please visit timberpress.com.

Library of Congress Cataloging-in-Publication Data

Beutler, Linda, author.
  The plant lover's guide to clematis/Linda Beutler.—First edition.
    pages cm
  Includes index.
  ISBN 978-1-60469-659-2
  1. Clematis. I. Title. II. Title: Clematis.
  SB413.C6B483 2016
  635.9'3334—dc23   2015029232

A catalog record for this book is also available from the British Library.

Mention of trademark, proprietary product, or vendor does not constitute
a guarantee of warranty of the product by the publisher or author and does
not imply its approval to the exclusion of other products or vendors.

Series design by Laken Wright
Cover design by Kristi Pfeffer
Printed in China

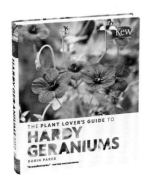

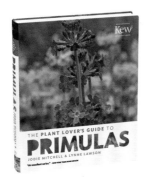